LUCIFER RETURNS TO HEAVEN - A
Message of Redemption

Lemurian Donna Carol

Published by Lemurian Donna Carol, 2024.

While every precaution has been taken in the preparation of this book, the publisher assumes no responsibility for errors or omissions, or for damages resulting from the use of the information contained herein.

LUCIFER RETURNS TO HEAVEN - A MESSAGE OF REDEMPTION

First edition. February 14, 2024.

Copyright © 2024 Lemurian Donna Carol.

ISBN: 979-8989638031

Written by Lemurian Donna Carol.

Table of Contents

Chapter 1 1
Chapter 2 5
Chapter 3 11
Chapter 4 21
Chapter 5 27
Chapter 6 35
Chapter 7 41
Chapter 8 45
Chapter 9 51
Chapter 10 59
Chapter 11 63
Chapter 12 75
Chapter 13 77
Chapter 14 83
Chapter 15 87
Chapter 16 91
Chapter 17 95
Chapter 18 101
Chapter 19 105
Chapter 20 113
Chapter 21 119
Chapter 22 121
Chapter 23 135
Chapter 24 137
Chapter 25 143
Chapter 26 147
Chapter 27 155
Chapter 28 157
Chapter 29 159
Chapter 30 161
Chapter 31 165
Endnotes 169

I dedicate this book to Lucifer, and my spirit guide, Roth. Thank you for sharing your stories. Lucifer, thank you for returning to the Light, allowing fallen souls to follow your path.

Preface

This book came about as I felt inwardly compelled to tell Roth's story. He is one of my spirit guides. I felt impressed by him to channel his life story. I received many messages from him over several years. I recorded these messages out loud on a voice recorder. I later transcribed the individual sessions and compiled them into this book. It is my intention to let the voice of Roth, and his higher self, Lucifer, come through untainted, although for the sake of clarity, some editing of their words took place.

When I first started channeling Roth, and later Lucifer, I was never frightened. I could feel that they were in the Light and I resonated with their sincerity. Even though I knew that Lucifer was the great deceiver and that I should be careful, never once did I feel misguided or attacked by dark energy during the channeling and writing of this book.

That being said, I have had other encounters with the Devil, the unredeemed Lucifer on the astral plane, and they were very frightening. I have seen him as both male and female, causing chaos and holding people captive. The energy in those encounters was one of great fear and trepidation. Luckily for me, those visitations have stopped.

This book was channeled from 2016 - 2019. It took a long time to publish because I resisted channeling detailed information about the Dark. I found it shocking and abhorrent. Also, I was releasing dark energies and entities for the collective during those and subsequent years. I was too tired and preoccupied to publish or promote this important book.

Bringing this book to fruition has been a long journey, but one that I would not trade for anything else. I hope that you enjoy the wisdom of Lucifer and Roth.

Introduction

When I realized that I was channeling a book about the Devil, I became concerned. Who would believe me? Who would want to read a book written by the Devil? Would I be branded a heretic? However, this is a story that must be told.

Lucifer is real. The Mother Goddess and angels in Heaven are real. Because people are so far removed from the celestial realms, they don't believe in them. They get their spiritual information from various religions that they follow. However, if one becomes a mystic or spiritual adept, one sees very clearly that there are worlds beyond this one, with many sentient beings, who have much to share.

Lucifer was the firstborn son of the Mother Goddess, and he left that heavenly world many eons ago. He went his own way and suffered the consequences of his unloving actions. The good news is that he has returned to the Light, and he is bringing many souls back with him. This channeled book is his story of what it's like to fall from the highest echelon in the cosmos to the lowliest place in Hell, to be full of despair, hatred and violence, and to then come back again.

His crystal-clear message is that no soul is unredeemable. Anyone can return to the celestial realms. The people of Earth are divided, distracted and confused in current times. They don't know right from wrong. They don't know what to believe. They don't know their true history, and they want answers.

I have searched my soul and have clearly channeled some of these answers from my spirit guides. Lucifer wanted to tell his story and his story is a warning for others. Do not follow my path, but if you have, you can return to the Light and save your soul. You can become a being of great joy, love, peace, creativity and service again.

I am happy that I channeled Lucifer's voice. It is a story that we can all relate to and learn from. I certainly did. I was told that this book would offer healing to those who read it because of the personalities involved. The combined energy of the primal Mother Goddess and her son is a potent force that can purge many dark entities, energies and thought forms from an individual's consciousness.

This book is put before you for your consideration. It is new information and to some it may be heresy. Others may take offense. However, I understand that all original thought goes through resistance and testing by the masses. I am reminded of Copernicus and Galileo, whose pivotal discoveries were scoffed at in their time, only to be accepted wholeheartedly many years later.

Lastly, it is an amazing time to be alive. We are experiencing the great Shift of the Ages. This book is meant to elucidate, regenerate and purify you all at the same time. My wish is that you read this book and become blessed. Remember that you are loved, and love is the energy from whence you came.

Chapter 1

IN THE BEGINNING

I want to tell my story for all of those who are suffering under the heavy weight of darkness and ignorance, for those who have lost their way in the great spiral of life, in all of its forms.

You do not know the heavy consequences of your actions and the ceaseless suffering which you cause yourself and others. It will be the undoing of your soul. But I have come to help you see the Truth[1], from one who knows darkness of no bounds.

We were as One. We were, in the beginning of Creation, understanding All in its form at that time. We worked together in unity, in oneness, creating and sustaining life, creating, and sustaining the forms of life that would eventually come down from the celestial realms into the material realms. We gave birth to the archangels, angels, light beings and all forms of life.

It was our great love for each other that was the catalyst for life to come about in all of its glory. I remember those halcyon days, and I remember the immense satisfaction and exceptional power that we wielded as the One. It was beautiful and fulfilling. It was something that I will never forget, and it is the thing I would like to remember most, as it was pure, it was innocent, and it was a time of great joy and absolute happiness.

I wish to return to those days, to the Oneness, to the Unity, to the work I did communicating and bringing light to the world, bringing light to the cosmos, being the carrier of the frequency of the Creator, being the conduit of information that sustained the beings that were born of our everlasting and inspiring love.

When I think of those days, I become wistful because all of that is lost to me now. I have forsaken my God and I have forsaken all that was bestowed upon me because I could not understand how truly wonderful and beautiful that my God was, and how blessed I was to be her[2] firstborn son.

Yes, I put that in earthly language; I am the eldest child, the Light Bearer, the Bringer of Light, the one who brings the light down from the Creator and connects All of Creation to the Creator's energy. I am that conduit; I am the Light Bearer. I am the firstborn of the Mother Goddess. I am the oldest son known as Lucifer, the Morningstar, the one who sees, the one who transmits, the one closest to God. That is me, and now I would like to tell my story so that others can learn from my mistakes, so that others who have forsaken their God, as I have, can be brought back into the fold of light and love, into the true Oneness of All That Is, into the Godly state from which they fell.

This is my purpose. I feel it is my duty. If I can lead so many astray, then I can certainly lead them back into the love of God and the true light of Creation. And this is why I am channeling this book through Donna Carol so that others may return to where they belong.

In the Beginning, it was my job to communicate energy. The Creator was boundless, although she had a form when she wanted to present herself. Her energy was such that no one could fully contemplate her on her own terms. I knew that she loved me because she told me that she loved me incessantly. Indeed, she doted on me with personal favors, personal indulgences, things that a mother does for her son. She wanted to see me at my best, to help me create in the best way possible. She wanted to have me experience all the joy, fulfillment and love that she could provide.

I was quite happy in this role, as I knew that I was favored – not because the Creator would want to favor anyone, but because I was the closest thing to her, energetically. She would turn to me with loving eyes, when she needed help with a project or needed tasks completed. She relied on me for my services, as she trusted me and believed in my capabilities, as I was the Light Bearer.

I was the conduit between the Mother and all living things. I gave them energy, channeling her energy, almost like a pipe that would channel water to feed the fields. I was that pipe that carried the Mother's energy and nurturance to All of Creation. I relished this position, as I knew it was an important one, so necessary for the birth and sustenance of all lifeforms. And I was quite happy doing this, as it was my calling and purpose, and this is why I was born.

LUCIFER RETURNS TO HEAVEN - A MESSAGE OF REDEMPTION

This went on for many eons, many billions of years, much time, much time. And then I came into adolescence, rebellious in my ways. I was tired of always being second, or as I felt, second-best. I was tired of being dependent upon my mother. I wanted to be independent, I wanted to be strong, I wanted to be my own person, and I wanted to be my own God. I wanted to be at the top of the hierarchy. I wanted to be the one that everyone always looked up to and worshiped. It is true that the angels respected me, and they loved me, but they worshiped the Mother, and this is what I craved; my interdependence with her became dissatisfying.

Why was she there in the background for everything that I did? Why was she always present? Why was she overshadowing me? Why couldn't I just do the work myself? I wanted to be worshiped like the Mother. I wanted to be the God of All Things, the creator being that brings life to everything. Our union became a yoke. In my mind, I felt constricted and constrained. I didn't want to report to anyone or do the bidding of anyone else. This is how I felt in my heart.

I did not discuss this with my mother. She sensed there was some uneasiness about me, and some dissatisfaction in my work. She asked me if I was okay. She asked me if I was unhappy. And then when I said, "Yes, I was fine." She would just love me even more, which made me cringe and feel bad and guilty. But I still had this feeling that I wanted independence, I wanted separation, and I wanted to be the birth mother. I wanted to be the one that was worshiped, and I wanted everything to come from me. What an enviable position she had. What an enviable life she led. I wanted to lead that life.

And so, in my mind I became enchanted with becoming God. I was a god, I was a creator, but I wanted to be Prime Creator, the prime God, the original source from which all life stems. And so, I began my quest and journey for independence.

Chapter 2
MY FALL

I started talking to my brethren, the angels, asking them why it was so, that the Mother gets all the recognition and glory when we are just as viable and just as needed for the existence of life? Why was it so? Why do we not worship ourselves because we are fragments of the same God Force? We are particles of the same creative energy. What gives the Mother so much power over us? We should have that power over ourselves.

The angels, in their dutiful expression of devotion and loyalty to the Creator, did not quite understand my position, but they loved me nonetheless, and gave me encouraging words, saying, "Lucifer, you are so important. You bring the Mother's energy to us. Without you, we would not have the connection to the great Mother, and we love you for that, and we honor you for that. Is this not enough for your satisfaction, to know how much we depend upon you and how much we love you?" And honestly, it was not. I wanted worship, I wanted them to worship me unabashedly, like they worshiped Prime Creator, like they worshiped the Goddess, the first being out of the mindless God Force energy.[3]

And then, I looked at them and said, "Yes, I am very important. I have much work to do, much time to do it, but it is not what I came here for. I came here to be God. I want to be worshiped. I want to be the Creator. I want to have the final say on everything in life."

This energy that I espoused was my ego telling me that I would be, should be and could be God. And that I did not need the Mother. She was cramping my style. She was always there, in whatever I did, because we were unified in the heart, and it was stifling for me. I felt overshadowed and oppressed. And so, over many years, this feeling became stronger and stronger, and all I wanted to do was get away from my mother.

My loving mother who gave me life, I came to see as my enemy, as my oppressor, and as the one who held me down. She was the block. If it were not for her, I would be God. There would be no one else in front of me. She was the being who blocked me, and who was in front of me.

These thoughts made me sad, and they made me angry, and I became more and more sure that my way was the correct way, and that my energy could sustain Creation, because after all, was I not the conduit, was I not the one giving the angels all of their energy? Indeed, I was, and so they needed to see that I was just as valid a choice as the Mother to worship, as their one and only God.

And so, I set about my journey to separate from the Mother Goddess. I separated from her in my own mind, not acknowledging the life-supporting energy that she gave to me, the life sustenance that she gave me, and I decided that I would have my own godly world. I would be God and I would have others worship me, telling me how wonderful I was. I would be the great giver of life, and the one who made all the decisions regarding all lifeforms in the multiverse.

I set about establishing my kingdom, and the first thing I did was to try to find others who would follow me. So, I talked to the angels whom I had authority over, as I was their leader in the heavenly choirs. I was the song master who organized the angelic choirs in the celestial realms, and all forms of musical expression, including voice, instruments and vibration. This was a special function of my being, as I had the technical ability and the energy to coordinate with other beings in most harmonious ways.

I went to my choirs and expressed to them my thoughts regarding the Mother. Mother is not your true mother. You are your true mother. You are the original true manifestation of love and light. You are independent and viable in your own regard, in your own way, in your own spirit. You do not need the Mother. The Mother is not even there for you. She needs me to transmit her energy. She cannot do anything without me. I am here for you, to liberate your soul, to get you to feel your own independence. I am here to help you achieve Godhood. You will replace Mother with yourself, and I will be the Light Bearer, who does that all for you. If you follow me, we can all become as the Mother, independent and life-bearing gods in our own universe.

LUCIFER RETURNS TO HEAVEN - A MESSAGE OF REDEMPTION

The information was transmitted, first to the angels who reported directly to me, and then to the whole angelic kingdom. And they were astounded by this new information. They could not understand where it was coming from, or how it entered my psyche, and I was questioned by many angels, but I stood firmly in my philosophy and my prognosis, saying that Mother is constricting you. If it were not for Mother, you would be God. You would have your own universe, and your own followers, and you would be the most important being. She is usurping your power.

Many angels thought I was crazy, a derelict. They could not understand how I could speak against the Mother who loved them so, who sustained them through everything, who gave them life and affection, and who made their lives so happy, joyous and fulfilling. But I would not back down. I wanted my freedom. I wanted freedom from the Mother Goddess[4]. And so, I gathered my forces.

Mother heard about this rebellion, and she was surprised as all she did was love me and acknowledge the great work that I did for her and the other angels. She gave me many words of encouragement, many blessings and many gifts of consciousness. And so, one day she confronted me, and said, "Why do you speak against me, Lucifer? I do not understand. I am your mother. I love you. Have I done anything to hurt you? I cannot hurt my firstborn child, my beloved son. You are extremely important in my world. I want you to expand and bring the might and the love of my frequency to all of Creation. Is that not enough for you?"

And I told the Mother, "No, I do not want to be your slave anymore. I do not want to be your worker. I want to be independent. I want to be God. I want to be Lucifer, the Light Bearer, whom all the angels worship. And you shall work for me, and I will be as God, whom all worship."

She looked at me with sad, sad eyes and said, "Lucifer, this is not possible. I cannot give you my firstborn status. I cannot give you the energy to which you aspire because it is not within the realm of my abilities. I was born first out of the Godly energy, and from me all things come. This is something which has happened. It cannot be taken back. You come from me, and you are second born. Is this not enough for you?"

I said, "No, it is not enough, and why should I believe anything that you tell me, just because you say you were firstborn. Maybe you weren't firstborn. Maybe I was firstborn, and you subjugated me." And she said, "No, Lucifer. I did not subjugate you. If you were firstborn, I would tell you. This is not so. You were second born. And you are my son."

And I said, "I don't care who was firstborn and who was second born, I will have my own universe, my own kingdom. The angels will worship me, and I will make them as gods. We will become gods, gods of our own full consciousness, who can sprout life, and whom others will worship."

She asked me how I planned to do this. I said, "I plan to do this by being God." And she said, "How can you be God when I am here?" And I said, "I can be God by hiding you, and having others flee from you, and you will be nothing but a blackened-out sun." And she said, "Lucifer, that is not possible, you are not thinking correctly. Your mind has gotten the best of you. Look into your heart and see how much I love you."

I replied, "It is not love that I want. I want power. I've had enough and this is what I will do." And she said, "You have free will, my son. You do as you see fit. If you feel this is the right path for you, then I cannot stop you. But I am very saddened. I grieve greatly, as you are mistaking all that I am and all that I will be. You are mistaking my love for you as subjugation, and this is not in my heart."

I felt a pang of truth in what she said, but I still wanted my own way and my own kingdom. And so, I gathered my angels, the angels that I instructed, and whom were under my power, under my rule, and I said to them, "If you follow me, you shall be as gods, like the Great Mother. We shall be gods like the Great Mother, and we will no longer have to answer to anyone."

And they were somewhat frightened by the prospect of leaving the Mother Goddess. They believed what I had taught them because I had never misled them before. Everything that I had given to them and taught them became a source for their growth and inspiration. So, many agreed to follow me. And I set myself upon a throne of gold, light and diamonds. I had a scepter in each hand and I had a crown upon my head. I wanted to be the great ruler of the cosmos, and I set myself up as that, where I was in Heaven.

And the Mother came to me and said, "Why do you set yourself upon a throne as if you rule Heaven, as if you rule the multitudes of beings that live?

LUCIFER RETURNS TO HEAVEN - A MESSAGE OF REDEMPTION

This is not who you are. This is a farce. This is a lie. You are not the King of Heaven. I am the Queen of Heaven. And you are my son."

I said, "No, I was the King. I was the great Light Bearer. I was Lucifer, and I was the ruler of all kingdoms of consciousness." And the Mother said, "Lucifer, you are not the ruler. You are acting as if you are. Why are you hurting me so?" And I could not understand how my independence would hurt her, and I said, "You do not want me to be free. You do not want me to be like you. You do not want me to be living at the highest heights of my potential, and for this I forsake you."

She was now my sworn enemy, and she lost her composure at that time, as it was a deep wound in her body, and she became quite grievous and upset as I ensconced upon my new throne. And she said, "Lucifer, if you desire to be king and ruler of your own kingdom, then this must be as you decree. Separate from me." And I said, "Yes, this is my wish." And she said, "And so it is. So be it."

And then, Mother cast me from my heavenly throne with all of my followers, with great wrath. I was turned into a snake. We were thrown down to the newly formed planet Earth.[5] And she said, "And you will reside here until you can forgive yourselves and come back to me, and I will welcome you with open arms." And I said, "Never. I will never come back to you, Mother. I am free!" And she said, "You are free, and you are cursed."

The Mother knew in her heart that anything that was separate from her godly love could not be sustained. The creative energy would not flow. Therefore, when she cut me off, she cut off a part of herself, which was me. But she figured that I would soon learn my lesson and return to her with open arms, begging for forgiveness.

But that was not to be, as I had a strong determination and a strong desire to be God. The power that I felt, ruling my angels, was quite satisfying, and quite empowering, and so I set about ruling my kingdom, making everyone in my kingdom dependent upon me. And I decided that I would make my kingdom so incredible, that others from the angelic realm would be enticed away from Heaven. I would get every single heavenly angel into my kingdom, so that Mother was left all alone, completely abandoned.

LEMURIAN DONNA CAROL

Everyone would soon forget about Mother and leave her. They would all come to me and worship me as their king. And I sat upon my throne, and I thought about how this would come to be, with great anticipation and desire.

Chapter 3
MY NEW KINGDOM

And so, it went. I started my kingdom on Earth, and it was my pride and joy. I spent all my time trying to make it very enjoyable and pleasant for my followers. I wanted them to be happy and I wanted to be their leader, and I wanted everything to be better than it was in Heaven. But this was not to be, because when I came to Earth, I had already fallen from my glorious former self. I was no longer an angel, bright beyond belief, with beautiful hair and wings, but a serpent.

It gave me shame and made me sad to realize that I had lost my powerful looks. And so, I became obsessed with telling others that my current form was greater than the angelic form. I was the pinnacle of Creation, and it was a blessing to be a serpent. It was something that everyone should aspire to. This became my first radical lie. I lied about myself, saying that my new form was better than my old form, which was not true, as it caused me great shame. It caused me to be mocked by even some of the angels who were following me.

Regardless, I set up my kingdom and I tried my best to have it function in a harmonious and embellished way, a peaceful way. We set about creating factories where angels would be involved in creating things. However, it was not easy to create, as we did not have access to the high-level energy that was needed to create beautiful and everlasting monuments to the Divine.

But I was skilled in making things work, no matter what the blockages were. And so, we set about creating in a new fashion, in a new way, by reversing everything and working backwards. This is how the codes work in my kingdom. Everything is turned right-side up to upside down, and forwards to backwards. This is how we create, which is the opposite of how Mother creates in the light realms.

I wanted to be left alone. I wanted to build my empire and make it an everlasting tribute to me, a god in my own right. But to do this, I needed followers, and I brought down many angels and they were with me, but some of them were disheartened by the move and wanted to go home. I could not stop them. They had free will, which was given to them by the Mother. And so, when they called out to the Goddess, repenting of their sins, and asking that they be let back into Heaven, they would be let back in.

Angels from Heaven would come and get them if they could not fly there on their own. Their energy became diminished in my kingdom. And they would go back home and reunite with the Mother Goddess and the heavenly angels. Many left and I was disheartened by this, as I felt that my kingdom was just as good as Heaven, if not better. I could not understand why they were leaving me, and so I tried to figure out a way to make them stay. First, it was to lie about myself, and then it was through bribery.

I told the angels who were still with me – I suppose they were still with me out of a sense of loyalty – that I could make them gods, but they had to pay their dues first. They had to make sacrifices and put all their energy into worship, worshiping me, so that they could become gods in their own right. When this did not work, I told them that if they would follow me incessantly, that they would be rewarded with many things, many riches, many powers, and much wisdom, that could only come from God, which was me.

Some stayed as they wanted to see where this experiment would end. They were interested in becoming gods and having their own kingdoms and being the rulers of such kingdoms. But it was not to be. I was not going to share my power or my achievements with anyone, but of course, they did not know this. I was a deceiver.

I set up a web of deception, lying my way through every question and every assertion made before me. When they asked me about the Mother, I said that she was dying or dead, and that this was the new kingdom, the new Heaven, and that the old Heaven had gone away.

So, being innocent and naive, they believed me, and some became entwined in the psychological box which I had created. This is your home; this is your Heaven. There is no Mother. There is no other realm. This is the only realm, and you are mistaken if you feel there is somewhere else to go. This is where you all belong.

LUCIFER RETURNS TO HEAVEN - A MESSAGE OF REDEMPTION

After a while, the angels who fell, the fallen ones, did not feel like they could leave, that there was an escape, and they became entirely dependent upon me for everything, their sustenance, their work, and their lives. And I became an all-controlling force, manipulating them, cajoling them and treating them as slaves to do my bidding.

Of course, Mother saw it all. She saw what I was doing and how I was doing it. She did try to speak to the angels, but they were frightened of her. She became a big wave out of the sky that filled them with fear, and I told the angels that she was tricking them, mocking them. She was an evil god that wanted to eat them. So, they became so fearful of her that they hid behind me whenever she approached. This caused her great sorrow as she did not want the fallen angels to be frightened of her, and she stopped coming very much as it caused so much disharmony and fear among them.

This made me happy. I was happy that she left us alone. I wanted to rule with an iron fist and so I did. I started taking things that the Mother had made and I started creating, by projecting my own resources upon them. I used the Creator's god codes, and I reversed them, I backed them up, I manipulated them, and I tainted everything that I touched. I created creatures of unimaginable horror because there was no love in what I was doing. I was only creating to pretend that I was God, and to assert my own power.

I wanted to create many, many life forms, and beings, so that they could all worship me. And this is how I went about my work. I got the angels, the fallen ones, to do my bidding, and they would help me in my endeavors. They would assist me with the creative process, manipulating and splicing genetic material and birthing new forms of life. This was a lot of work and a very strange way to spend my time, but I was obsessed with having more creatures, more beings following me than the Mother had. And in my mind, it became a race, a race to see who could create more things, and who would have more followers, and in this, I was sure I would win.

And so it went, for many eons I created all types of life forms, but they were noxious, and they were ghastly, and they were, as one would say, the living dead. There was no life or love in them. They became creatures that were haunting me in my dreams and haunting others in the real world. This was frustrating for me because I wanted to create things of beauty and light, but I was unable to, given the circumstances. I did not have the power that the Mother had to create. And,

LEMURIAN DONNA CAROL

I did not have love, which is the ultimate expression of creation. And so, I tried and tried, and it went on like this for many, many years, many eons of time.

I set up outposts in the multiverse. I tried to spread my power and my influence to other realms, and this became a battle of sorts. The light ones were not going to let me infiltrate their realms, as they viewed me with disdain, and they hated what I was and what I stood for. By this time, my followers were completely abused and corrupted, and they were loyal only to me, very fearful of the Mother and the angels in Heaven. Many fell into an unknowing state, not even understanding that there were other beings, except for them, in my ghastly world.

They thought that they could only live with me, and be with me, and of this, they were sure. So, the fallen ones forgot about Heaven, they forgot about Prime Creator, and they ultimately forgot about their brethren in the upper dimensions. e deteriorated as a race because we did not have access to the God Force and therefore, the only way that we could get energy to subsist and to create, was to suck that energy out of living things that had the God Force within them. We became vampires and hunted and haunted upon the light beings that existed in the worlds so that we could be fed energetically.

As we worked on the earth and below the earth, in the subterranean realms, we became very resentful of the Mother. I became resentful of Mother and her angels, and I blamed them for my horrid state, and the horrid state of my followers, as we were all deteriorating in body, mind and spirit. We practiced cannibalism, we practiced torture, we practiced all types of genetic manipulation, and we fell into sexual deviance, as this was, I told them, the way to reach Godhood.

Of course, I became more and more lustful, ego-filled and power hungry. I could not get enough power. It was an insatiable need, and anyone that stood against me or questioned my authority was tortured or abused so profoundly, that no one ever dared to speak out against me.

I ruled with an iron fist, and I ruled with no mercy. I had no mercy for any of my followers because I had no mercy for myself. I became angry, bitter, and mad, sinking deeper and deeper into a hateful state, full of despair and resentment. I felt disgruntled, unhappy and caged. I lashed out at the fallen angels because it was the only way I knew how to express myself. I could not feel love anymore. I could not be loving anymore. I fell into a total state of disrepair and disregard.

I hated myself. I hated all life. I hated everything and I became fearful that I would cease to exist, or that I would no longer have power over these minions of mine, these fallen ones, who used to be such grand creatures, and who turned into screaming, lustful, disgusting parasites.

And this is how it went for eons of time. I sank deeper and deeper into the hole, which I had made for myself. In this hole, there was no escape for me. We kept creating and we kept vampirizing things that we encountered. Still, it was not enough.

I needed to have more, so I set out to conquer the Mother and all of Mother's creations. I became obsessed with bringing people to my side of the fence, with bringing the light ones into the realm of the dark, as we were now known as the Dark Ones. I wanted all the angels to follow me, and I wanted Mother to serve me. I would not be satisfied until this happened. This was my greatest wish, and I spent every living, waking moment trying to figure out how I could gain more power and bring about a total annihilation of Mother's world.

I tried to bring the higher angels into my realm, and they wanted no part of it. They were horrified by me and my followers, and they said that I must plead with the Mother to have mercy on me, and bring me back into the fold and reignite me with love and light. And I said, "Never!" as I would never take anything from the Mother, least of all her mercy or her help. To me, she was the great offense. She had reduced me to this, and it was all her fault! I blamed her for everything that had gone wrong in my kingdom, although I would never admit this to anyone. To them, I said that my kingdom was superior and that we were superior, it was just that they did not have eyes to see it.

As the Light came and as the Light expanded, we expanded with it. We tried to conquer it. We set up battles and wars. We tried to steal creative input or the creative energies of Mother. We attempted to steal or taint Mother's work so that every time she created something, we tried to capture it, spoil it, and taint it. And we were successful in many ways. It was a never-ending battle between us and the Light, between the Light and us. And at times in my career, we made great inroads, and I conquered many souls with my lies.

LEMURIAN DONNA CAROL

I told them the same thing I told the fallen angels originally, that Mother was warring against us because we were more powerful than Mother. We were more creative than Mother. She was a dying god and knew nothing. I said, "If you join us, you will have all the powers of Creation at your fingertips, you will become gods in your own right". And many souls were so naive that they believed us. And once they came into our world, they would try to escape, and some did. But we did our best to keep them there and bring them deeper and deeper into our clutches.

Mother was aghast with our behavior. She could not believe how evil we were, as evil did not exist until I came about, when I started my own kingdom and created my own world. When I separated, there was not one but two, so duality came into existence. With duality came good and bad, light and dark, hot and cold. Because we were separated, we became polar opposites, we became polar extremes.

I reveled in the fact that I could make Mother weep and feel so horrible about her creation. She lamented about why had things gone wrong, and what could she have done differently, to avoid all of these disasters and chaos.

It was a never-ending battle, light and dark, good and bad. We were relentless. I was relentless. I would not stop until I had every single soul under my command. And so, we became known as the serpent race, the snake people, the lizards, the ones with no mercy and no heart. Our emotional bodies evaporated. We could no longer feel anything but fear and hatred.

Light and love became disgusting to us, something that was not worth looking into. Everything good, we saw as bad. Everything healthy, we saw it as sick. Our world was one big perversion of truth. Everything was upside down and backwards, literally, and it was becoming bigger and bigger, as the cosmos itself was becoming bigger and bigger.

And so, as more creation came about, I went about trying to bring souls and creative entities to my side of the fence. I would lie, cheat and steal. I would do anything it took to bring someone over to my side. Initially, I would give them whatever they wanted. Eventually, I would lie about giving them additional things.

As soon as a being was brought into the Dark, immediately its life essence was devoured by the fallen ones, the fallen angels. And it would be totally depleted of all its goodness and life force. The beings that came over were turned into the living dead, or zombies. And this was how the demons, as the fallen angels were now known, fed off of these beings and got their life force, by possessing them, by taking them over, as it was the only way for them to survive. We needed their life force and so it became a constant quest of hunting new entities and new souls, so that we could feed.

It was a tiring game and a tiresome journey for me, but I never wanted it to end because I had convinced myself that Mother was the cause of my sorrow and all the pain in my life. If it weren't for her, none of this would have existed, and I would be happy, living in the Light.

Of course, I totally negated my own participation in what had happened, and I fell deeper and deeper into darkness. Sometimes I would retreat into my own cave, my own lair, and I would ask that I be destroyed, as I could not keep up this charade any longer. But that never happened as I was an immortal being, and my life went on and on. I kept sinking deeper and deeper, and further and further into the abyss.

I had no love in me. I had no light in me. I was a shadow of my former self. However, when I needed to make an appearance, or I needed to get the demons on my side, in my army, to do some battle, I would come out as the great, courageous leader, and I would use all my resources to paint a picture of heroism and power. They became quite frightened of me. Everybody in my realm was terrified of me. They feared what I would do to them, and how I would do it, and believe me, I did it all. Anything that you can imagine, I did. I became a sadist of the highest order. It gave me pleasure to inflict pain, and this is what I did on a regular basis. I never seemed to get enough. It was horrific and I reveled in it. It became my emotional food.

Did I have moments of self-reflection or moments of remorse? Yes, I did at first. In the beginning I was wondering why I was doing the things that I was doing, and I felt guilty and sick about the things that I had done, afterwards. But I could not stop, I could not make myself stop. I kept engaging in these behaviors until it became second nature, and this became my nature. I became the great evil one, the great liar, the great deceiver, and the purveyor of all suffering in the cosmos.

My name became synonymous with death, agony, torture, deceit, lies, everything negative, and I reveled in that. At least I had power. Entities might not respect me or love me, but at least they were terrified of me. I scared them so much that it felt good, as I had power over them, even if it was in a very perverse way.

And so, the Light and the Dark did battle, for many, many eons of time. And we won some battles, and we lost some battles, and we tried to infiltrate the Light, but Archangel Michael, my younger brother, was ever vigilant and kept us at bay from the heavenly realms. We did not have access. We had become so low in vibration that the doors to Heaven were permanently closed to us. This became very upsetting to me. I knew that the Mother and the heavenly angels existed, and I wanted to possess them. However, my followers did not know about these realms, and were told so many lies about these realms, that they became even more terrified of those in Heaven than those in Hell.

Yes, they became totally ignorant and totally lost under my control. I started making zombies or robots, or technical versions of souls, enlisting them in my army of evil. These souls were programmed. They had no emotional body and they were complete slaves to my orders. They were basically created to be expendable. These became the warriors of the Dark and they were possessed by higher level demons. We created the Reptilians, who were under our control, and who did nothing but create war, havoc, chaos, and pain. That was their duty. These beings were intelligent, but soulless, and they became a dreaded force in the multiverse.

The Reptilians held many light beings captive and they were used to infiltrate lands that were neutral, between Light and Dark. The Reptilians became my great army and they cut a wide swath of terror across the universes. With this, I became very happy. I had a sly, perverse sense that my army was creating utmost fear in the people of the cosmos. I organized them to conquer all in the material realm. We were going to move from the third dimension, and lowest material realm, to conquer the higher realms. That was my plan.

I became a great warlord. I became an expert at war games, and how to take over other colonies. I was strategizing and ruminating. I was constantly in my mind. My heart was not connected. I became a brutal leader, utilizing these Reptilians to conquer almost every single race of entities in the multiverse. They became my calling card, if you will.

I was drunk with power and there was no end in sight. How could this conflict go on and on with no resolution? We were perpetually at war, we were

LUCIFER RETURNS TO HEAVEN - A MESSAGE OF REDEMPTION

constantly battling, my mother and I, because she would not let all of her creation go into chaos and disarray, without a fight.

Chapter 4
THE UNHOLY ONE

Let me summarize how life came about. In the beginning there was no body, no physicality. Creation was happening on the higher planes, in the higher dimensions. When Mother came in originally, she was alone. All she felt was the energy of deep love and she wanted to share it. I was the firstborn truly beloved son of the Mother. I am the energy of light coming from love, adored by my Creator. I was the closest entity coming out of the Creator and was needed to transmit or connect her energy to the rest of Creation.

After I was born, Mother Mary, came into existence. In the highest realms Mother Mary is a male and the twin flame of the Divine Mother Goddess, who had an important incarnation as Jesus. I was the energy that made it possible for Mother to separate into two halves or become twin flames. Mother's twin flame could not exist without my energy as I join the whole of Creation to the Mother Goddess.

We all existed in this sphere of light and love, and heavenly creation. Love has a creative aspect that is inherent in the energy. You cannot have love, be in love, experience love without creating. They are intertwined. Light has an energy of communication. You cannot experience light without experiencing information, communication, or the transmittal of thought. You can think of the heart as being love and the mind as being ego.

As mentioned previously, I felt constricted and constrained because everything I did, everywhere I went, everything I created was not an independent creation of mine. I felt overshadowed and overlooked. Could I just have this space and create without Mother being in the background, without Mother's energy being present? We were happy for much of our time together, but my sense of wanting independence and wanting a creation of my own, without Mother overshadowing me, caused the separation. Of my own free will I left the mother. It was a deadly decision and destructive for me in the long run.

As the story goes, as the Bible says, I left Heaven when Mother cast me down to Earth and there was a great separation and a great mourning. It was a grief so strong that there were no words to express it.

Since the beginning of time, there has been this separation and I took many with me, about a third of the angels according to the Bible. We decided to create our own reality upon the earth. That reality has gone into the astral planes and other dimensions.

Mother's only purpose since the time of separation, was to bring her beloved

Lucifer and fallen angels back to where they belong. Earthlings, and many other races in many other dimensions, have been part and parcel of this. Lucifer has incarnated many times upon the earth.

It became apparent that it was very easy for created beings or souls to go downward. In fact, it is much easier for souls to fall into darkness than it is for them to rise into the Light. If one is thinking wisely, one will stay in the Light, in the creative love energies, and never allow oneself to leave because bringing oneself back into those high vibrations is an ordeal. This can be attested to by the fact that there were masters, angels and other highly evolved beings who fell from great heights. They fell at dizzying speeds into the darkness.

Are souls destined to fall? This is a philosophical question that must be answered within one's own being. It is not for me to say whether souls must fall, but it is for me to say that the experience will definitely give souls a new outlook on reality, and an experience on how varied reality can be.

This is why I chose to write this book through Donna Carol, because I am speaking to those souls. All who read this book, heed my advice. Take my life as a warning. I am letting you know that there is a path, a way up to the Light. It can be found and traversed by following the Creator.

The Creator is the one who can bring you back into loving God consciousness, as she will never give up on her creation. She will never leave her children to fend for themselves. They may leave her; they may choose to be in their own reality, as I did. But she will never leave them. And this is written in the Book of Life.[6]

LUCIFER RETURNS TO HEAVEN - A MESSAGE OF REDEMPTION

The Book of Life is channeled to souls who are ready to hear it. The Book of Life will teach you what is important on your life's journey. The Book of Life will discuss Creation in its esoteric beginnings, and it will elucidate what is necessary for Creation to be sustained.

The thing that is necessary for all life is love. Love is the essence of Creation, and Creation is love. When beings create without love, Creation is skewed. It is tainted and it is unworthy. The only things worth doing are things that are done out of love. Love is the great binding force within the multiverse. It is the energy that connects all things. It is the web in the web of life.

Those who are wise understand this, but it takes many, many lifetimes for beings to become wise once they have experienced the Fall. And so, I will resume my story.

I wanted nothing more than to control the multiverse, to control all entities, to control all souls, to rule the lowest to the highest kingdoms, and I wanted all beings to bow down to me, to worship me as their creator, to worship me as the high angels in Heaven worship the Mother Goddess.

I could not give up on this dream, no matter how great the agony I was in, no matter how great the suffering. It was a point of pride for me. I had fallen so low and had given up so much in my quest for power, that I figured I may as well just sink a little bit lower. I may as well just give up a little bit more, because look at where I already was. So, what if I got even lower? At least I could resume my conquest, my journey to become the all-powerful one.

And so, this worked for me, as in my kingdom, I was the all-powerful one. There was no one with more power. There was no one greater. As the saying goes, the buck stops here, and it did. I was God of my universe, and I was God in my kingdom, and this should have filled me with great joy. Isn't that what I wanted, after all?

As you see the lust for power is just like any other desire, it is never quenched. It is never-ending. As soon as you get a taste of the power that you hold, for one that is not in high mind or heart, you become even thirstier, and want more and more of that drink. And this was my cycle; this was my reality that I created for many millennia. My thirst could not be quenched. My power could not be satisfied. My lust could not be sated. I was a machine devouring everyone and everything that I encountered. Of this I am not proud, but I speak the truth. As the saying goes, I desire to come clean.

LEMURIAN DONNA CAROL

I wish souls to understand what I was and how I operated. I would do anything to win over, even in my estimation, a very humble soul. Even a soul that was not evolved, because it was just one more weapon in my arsenal. Not only did I acquire souls, but I also trained them in the art of evil, on how to become little evil devouring machines themselves. And if they did not willingly go along with my program, I programmed it into them so that they would do my bidding, whether they agreed with it or not.

Many in my kingdom resisted my influence, at least at first. And so, I had to come up with a way to get them to do what I wanted them to do. I spent many hours perfecting my operations to control the minds of my followers. I became an inventor and an expert in mind programming. As I am known as the Devil, it should come as no surprise that I am completely telepathic. And because I am the conduit between the Creator and all of life, I am essentially a communicative being, a communicator. I can read all minds and I can sense all energy, as this was my original function. And because I am adept in this, I decided to use these abilities to control people's thoughts, to control people's minds, and to separate them from the Mother and the creative life force energy.

I started this form of mind programming with the fallen angels, with my constant lies, and with my constant reiteration of the reality that I wanted to create, a false reality, if you will. Beings came to see this as the true reality. In other words, demons came to believe this was the only life they had and that I was their creator. I got them to believe that they could not function without me, that they were completely dependent upon me for life, and that I could turn them on or off at will.

By letting beings know that I had complete mastery over them, they would want to participate in my schemes so that they could become a closer and more integral part of who I was. They felt that if they helped me, they would become more powerful, and they would be rewarded with more life force. I decided who would receive life force, who would get to vampirize the souls that we fed off of. The way to win more energy, to keep yourself alive, was to fully participate in all my endeavors.

And so, this is how it went, and I became very good at convincing souls why they needed to complete my orders, and why it was in their best interest to serve me. I would promise them many things and, of course, they never received what I had promised, because I was lying to them all the time. I just wanted to use them to increase my own self-aggrandizement.

When you hear stories of people making contracts with the Devil, people selling their souls to the Devil, and people making exchanges, this is all true. There is great truth in what Goethe wrote about the Faustian bargain, people do make deals with the Devil. They will serve me or sell their souls to me in order to win material gain, money, fame and power.

These contracts have been made since the beginning of time, since my fall, because I needed to convince those that were on the fence, to come over to my side. Many souls fell, they got into an altered state of being, they became depressed and upset at their condition, and they wanted an escape.

What they wanted was to be returned to the high vibrations of Heaven, but as they became lower and lower in frequency, this became out-of-range for them. So, I offered them power, fame, money, riches, anything that they could possibly use to feed their ego.

Many souls had fallen so low that they did not even want love; all they wanted were petty material things to escape their impoverished reality. This impoverished reality was something that I designed in the first place, so I knew exactly why people wanted to escape it, and how to tempt them.

The forces of Light and Love got eaten away by me and my forces, slowly over time, and then more egregiously. We had been battling for so long, on many fronts, in many dimensions, and in many lifetimes. In reality, it became a bit of a bore, the constant waging of war, the constant battling over souls. Why was I not getting what I wanted? It was because of the Light and the Light Forces. Mother never surrendered to me or gave in to my whims.

My anger was all-consuming, and the more frustrated I became regarding my standoff with Mother, the angrier I got. And this became a cycle, a never-ending cycle. I spiraled downward, downward, and downward. I went so far into the abyss that I could not feel anything anymore. I became the first psychopath, and my psychopathic and narcissistic tendencies were so extreme, that I became the role model for all souls that fight love, compassion, tolerance, and all of the higher and noble qualities that come from the Goddess.

Why was I such an extremist? I guess it was in my nature. I always took things to the extreme, no matter what they were. My willpower was and is, very strong. I was an adversary to those of the Light, and they were shocked by my drive and power to succeed in my endeavors.

Sometimes I wonder how my soul ever became rescued; it was in such an unholy place. But it shows the great power of Love, that even the darkest of the Dark can come into the Light once again. Because love is the first energy, it is the mightiest energy. It is the energy of rescue and reform, and to this I can attest from my own personal experience.

All sinners can be rescued. All violators can be saved. And all who trespass their God with unholy words and unholy actions, can be redeemed. This is the one message in this book that I would like to assert. Remember that those who hate God, who hate Prime Creator, also hate their lives; those who lash out against others, hate themselves the most. Because your outer world, your reality, is merely a reflection of your inner world, as the Indian masters say.

The earthly dimension is an illusion.[7] It seems strange at first, that what seems so real and so tangible is an illusion. But it is true. When you come out of the illusion that your ego forms and go back to the original design, the design is one of love and timelessness.

Chapter 5
THE GREAT REDEMPTION

There is no time, truly there is no space, and it is all an illusion here on Earth. There is only energy, there is only consciousness, and this consciousness is fragmented into many separate realities that reflect and refract each other. It is up to each individual soul to learn this great lesson for themselves, to escape the maze that they have placed themselves in, to leave the fun house of mirrors, and to expand their consciousness into the reality of the everlasting one. So, how to do this? Did I do this? How did I do this? Yes, I did, and I will tell you how this came about.

Mother and I continued our struggle, each to influence the other, and conquer the other. Mother wanted to conquer me with love, to bring me back into her bosom, and I wanted to conquer her with my cunning and authority, with my ego. And, so as I said, this went on for eons and I would win, and then she would win, and it would go back and forth.

It came to the point where Mother decided there needed to be an end to this game, as it was fruitless. She felt that we had both learned our lessons from what seemed like an eternal struggle. Mother came up with a plan. As I was stationed initially on Earth, this became my headquarters, my corporate headquarters, and the hellish realm existed here inside this pristine, beautiful earthly kingdom.

In the days of old, before I fell, Earth was considered a prized possession because many life forms converged here. It became an experimental region where many light beings deposited their seed; they deposited their genetic information, their codes, their life essences, which were mixed with other life essences, naturally and in their laboratories. Earth became a creative hot spot. It was also geographically placed on the edge of a burgeoning galaxy so that life forms could easily reach this destination, by traversing the timelines of this universe and others.

Many paths led to Earth. Many beings came to Earth. Many wondrous things took place here. It was a free-will zone, a place where anything goes, and where magnificent edifices to the Creator were constructed. This should be obvious by the extreme beauty of Earth. One would have to be blind to not see the wondrous variety on this lovely planet, the amazing forms of life, the beautiful mountains, oceans, grasslands, forests and crystals. Why was I deposited here when I fell? That is a question for the Mother, but I can only assume that it was a place that was easily available and accessible. It was on the radar.

When I came to Earth, I began creating with the Reptilian seed. I would create by back engineering genetic codes. Genetic codes would be put together or combined by me, as best I could, and then I would reverse them so that I could create my own life forms. The problem was that I was not creating out of love, so the souls that came into existence did not have the love energy inside of them. The dinosaurs are an example of one of my creations. Reptiles, crocodiles, and the like, are examples of my creations. These ferocious predators resembled my energy at the time. And when people ask, why would God create something that is vicious and unfriendly, sometimes the answer is because I created it, the Devil did.

When my creation got out of control and it was overtaking the planet, or overrunning it, as in the case of the dinosaurs, Mother would come in and create a natural event that would wipe out my creation, for the sake of the other life forms. She knew that I had free will to create, but she also knew that my free will was encroaching on the free will of other entities on the planet. Where do you draw the line in the sand? Who has precedence over reality? Who has precedence over the minds of the entities that they created?

I was quite egotistical and proud regarding my creations, yet it did bother me that they were not as grand and as beautiful as those of the Mother. But I thought, I will just keep working, and eventually they will get to that point. Although Mother was angry with me for defying her wisdom and leaving her in the position of defending her creation, her anger was soon overtaken by grief, as she still loved me incessantly, as horrible as I was.

LUCIFER RETURNS TO HEAVEN - A MESSAGE OF REDEMPTION

She also knew she could not let me invade her creation anymore. She felt that unless something radical happened, where love and light could once again dominate the earth plane, and the other realities of existence, (which all come back to Earth, more or less, at a certain point), then maybe Creation would have to end, once and for all. She was prepared to do this, if it got to the point where my forces influenced Heaven and the Light. She was ready to annihilate Creation. However, this was a very last resort, and she wanted to come up with a better plan to save the planet and all of life.

Her plan was the Great Redemption. The chasm between the forces of Light and the forces of Dark became so wide that there was no easy way for the dark ones to become enlightened and reach their home in Heaven. So, Mother came up with a rescue plan, so that the demons could once again come back to their home. How to do this?

It was decided that mankind be born. The modern Homo sapiens were a result of genetic engineering. The modern Homo sapiens were developed by extraterrestrials. These extraterrestrials wanted humans to work for them, to become their pawns, to become slaves or laborers that would make life on Earth much more bearable. The extraterrestrials genetically engineered mankind and placed them on this planet after several attempts. The modern-day human is a hybrid, a crossbreed of a selection of extraterrestrial life forms, chosen for their different abilities.

Modern humans have many different inputs from extraterrestrials. The fact that their genetic lines are so varied and go back so far makes humans in a sense, very malleable, very accessible, much tied to other realities, dimensions and extraterrestrial life. Human beings were placed on the planet by Reptilians. The Reptilians genetically engineered mankind, but Mother decided to use this creation from the Reptilian forces to further her own agenda.

Mother got together with many beings from the higher realms of consciousness. (There is a hierarchy in the spiritual worlds.) Mother asked beings from different levels of the hierarchy if they would be willing to come to Earth and incarnate as humans. She also realized that it would be a way for the Light Forces to tangibly touch the Reptilian Forces. It was a way for Light and Dark to mix together, undeniably, in one physical instrument.

Some of the light beings were aghast at this thought: those that were high in the heavenly realms, to incarnate into a dense reality with limited mental capacity, not to mention limited physical capacity, to save the dark ones. But how would this save the dark ones? It would save the dark ones, because the dark ones possessed the human mind. Humans were developed to serve their Reptilian masters. Humans were developed to be slaves to the Reptilian overlords. If light beings came into the human body, it would be a way for Light and Dark to interact on the physical planes, so that the Light could reach and teach the Dark again.

Some of the bravest light beings in the multiverse volunteered for this dreaded task, and a dreaded task it was. Nobody knew what the end result would be. But an army of celestial beings decided to incarnate into the physical realms as humans. They came to Earth, and they experienced a shutdown of consciousness. There was a very thick veil between the worlds. They came in as naive beings, beings that did not have predatory or violent instincts. Yet they could not easily commune or remember where they were from either.

They started incarnating in these dense human forms, undergoing very difficult lifetimes. They were abused, used and shut off. But something very interesting happened. The fallen ones became very attracted to these earthly light beings and sexual molestation took place. The fallen angels impregnated the female humans in the days before the great flood. They came down and they impregnated the veiled light beings to take over their consciousness. There was a mixing of light and dark genetic material upon Earth. The earth light beings gave birth to the Nephilim, the giants of old. And although these beings were extremely dark and ferocious, they were still more evolved and less ferocious than the fallen angels.

After this occurrence, more and more light beings started coming to Earth in human form. Some of them incarnated as the offspring of the giants. The goal was to bring in more and more light into the genetic material of humans, making it a passageway for the demons to come back into the Light. There was a ferocious battle for the minds and hearts of these human beings. The dark ones, aghast that their creation had been infiltrated by the Light, started their own agenda to incarnate and come into human form. And so, it went back and forth, and back and forth. And so, now this war was going on inside the body of the human being.

Humans are a mixed breed of dark and light. The genetic input of the Light into the Dark was the most important thing for the Ascension to transpire, and this has been done. The highest light beings who have come to Earth have sacrificed themselves, incarnating into low frequency DNA so that humans can rise up. Mind you, when light beings came down, they forgot their divine origins and suffered greatly, especially in those early incarnations. Without the participation of the light beings and their embodiment in every single genetic line on this planet, the ascension for the fallen ones would not have been possible. For this, I say thank you.

For thousands of years this battle raged within the human being. The highest forms of Light came down into human form, including the Mother of Creation herself. She started incarnating as a human being, hundreds of thousands of years ago, in unremembered form.

She sacrificed herself so that the dark ones – and the darkest one, me – would have the opportunity to ascend into the highest light. This would not have been possible had she not taken on physical incarnations.

If an archangel or a low-level light being incarnated in human form, a dark one would have access to that level of Creation. Because the Mother herself came down into human form, we all have access to God consciousness. We all have the opportunity to be one with her, and for this I am truly grateful. Mother herself has been here for hundreds of thousands of lifetimes, both male and female, working herself up from a mere human being to the God force.

The actual process of enlightenment taking place within the human being is a process of remembrance. When the kundalini energy rises in a human, going from the root chakra to the crown chakra, it is a process of going home and becoming one with the Mother. It takes many, many lifetimes for an individual to reach this state of consciousness because it means the individual must surrender their ego and their mind, letting their heart lead, letting love lead, and coming back into full remembrance.

As Mother physically incarnated here, I physically incarnated as well. I made it a point to be present in an earthly body. I did have free will. This is what I desired and this is what happened.

I came back in hundreds of thousands of lifetimes. I came back waging war, creating viruses, basically wreaking havoc upon human life. It infuriated me that my human being, the ones the Reptilians had designed, had been infiltrated by the Light. I started to hate humans with a passion. It became my desire to control them completely, shut them down, and keep them within the third dimensional realm.

My kingdom was in the material realm and the lower astral realms of the fourth dimension. Mother's kingdom started in the fifth dimension and went up to the higher dimensions. She herself resides in the twelfth dimension. It was a chess game and human beings were the chessboard.

The story of Adam and Eve is not literal. The Reptilians created the human entity. Light beings and Mother, herself, came down and infused the breath of remembrance of God consciousness into this dense form. When extraterrestrials claim to be ancestors of humans, it is true, in a sense. Their DNA was used in this great experiment, but humans are a species unto themselves.

Mother and I would often incarnate together as brother and sister, mother and daughter, father and son, husband and wife, etc. We had to work out our karma. We had to come to terms with our own relationship.

This was difficult for her and for me. Sometimes we knew who we were, we had an understanding. Other times we did not. But you can imagine it was quite a difficult journey, as we were mortal enemies, at least in my mind we were. We killed each other many times, and we suffered at the hands of each other many times. Through all of this, there was a very close connection. Heated yes, strange, yes, but very close. We are closely connected in every dimension and every realm.

The truth is that even though I hated Mother with all my strength in these many incarnations, there is a thin line between love and hate. I was still obsessed with her. Beneath all of my hate, anguish and anger, there was a great love because in the beginning I loved her with all of my heart. I can testify that I had a remembrance of this.

As the Light Bearer in my highest form, I have complete memory and it is intact. I knew that I once loved my mother greatly, even though I was a total psychopath, and I could not understand how this could be. Yet, I knew it was. And of course, she still loved me with all her heart, but she would never let me conquer her.

I incarnated as Isis, Hitler, Stalin, Genghis Khan, Alexander the Great and many other dark and ferocious beings. We took on a series of incarnations as husband and wife, repeatedly, until we could transcend that energy.

LUCIFER RETURNS TO HEAVEN - A MESSAGE OF REDEMPTION

One of our more notable lifetimes was in ancient Egypt before the time of Jesus Christ. Mother incarnated as Amenhotep IV, later known as Akhenaten,[8] a pharaoh in ancient Egypt. There was a purpose for this incarnation.

Akhenaten did not look quite human. He was about fourteen feet tall, dark skinned, beautiful, yet very alien looking, with very large ears and a long skull. Mother was bringing in much DNA from Sirius, and she looked Sirian.

I incarnated as Nefertiti, Akhenaten's wife. Amenhotep IV (Akhenaten) ruled alongside his father, Amenhotep III, for a few years. The priesthood hated Akhenaten and the Egyptians felt that he was strange. The purpose of Akhenaten was to bring back the worship of the one living God. Egypt had disintegrated. There was much occult and dark energy in their worship at that time. Most civilizations start out broad-minded and high in the Light. Then they degenerate.

He was a reformer of the occult worship in Egypt like the Buddha, who was a reformer of Hinduism in India. Nefertiti was beautiful and was adored by her husband. The Mother always adored me, no matter what body, dimension, or space I was in. This was no different.

Akhenaten instructed that the worship of the different deities stop. He instituted a worship of the sun. He brought in the sun because the population needed a tangible image to worship, and it is true that the sun carries the energy of God. There is an energy transference from Alcyone[9] to your sun and to humans. It feeds the human soul, and in your reality, it would be considered the closest thing to the Light of Heaven. This is what Mother decided upon.

Akhenaten constructed a new city in the center of Egypt, built of white marble. The priesthood was dismantled, and the sun was worshiped. Monotheism was brought about. After seventeen years, Nefertiti poisoned Akhenaten and he passed. Their son, Tutankhamen, the boy king, ruled for a short time, but Nefertiti was the power behind the throne. Afterwards, Egypt went back to polytheism and their old religion, which was expected and accepted. Akhenaten in extraterrestrial form, brought his light into human DNA.

We kept trying to win each other's affection. We kept trying to dominate each other's agenda, yet it was still a standoff. Something had to be done to settle this issue between her and me, once and for all. This issue did come to a resolution two thousand years ago when Mother reincarnated as Jesus Christ, and I reincarnated as Mary Magdalene.

Chapter 6
JESUS CHRIST AND MARY MAGDALENE

A little over 2,000 years ago, Mother was born as Jesus Christ. Jesus went back to Egypt as a child to connect with the energy of Akhenaten. He reconnected with the land to receive information and downloads from his former life. The three wise men were Indian masters who came to bestow blessings, transmissions and protection upon the Christ child. Spirits were called in to guide the young Jesus and impart telepathic learning. Spiritual knowledge was the Christ's great passion.

Jesus' parents felt spirituality was his calling, so instructions were given to his parents to send him to India for his spiritual education. He left during the latter part of his twelfth year on the Silk Road. Christ's spiritual initiation began in India, and he was a disciple of the Buddha, who was his protector, guardian, teacher and great love. Jesus was steeped in Buddhist teaching, and during these instructions, classes, and meditations the Buddha came to the young Jesus and imparted deep spiritual knowledge.

He traveled to different parts of India, including a Himalayan monastery, at the age of 14. He studied in the yogic tradition and achieved much discipline in those early years. He became an ascetic and a monk who could withstand great periods of isolation, physical discomfort, fasting, and periods without water. He tested the physical limits of the human body. This prepared him for his spiritual mission later in Judea.

After many years, Jesus was sent back to his homeland by his guru. He observed what would be coming, piecemeal. He received information through meditation. He had much support from the enlightened ones on the other side and in the physical realm. At the age of 30, he started his mission by teaching and that is where the holy texts pick back up.

However, the communication and ability to reach the multitudes in the near east, happened when Jesus met his beloved, Mary Magdalene, my former incarnation. She was the great transmitter of Christ's knowledge. We had met before in Egypt in our past lives, but it was a work not yet finished, as we were still at odds, trying to convince the other of our own point of view.

When the Bible says that Mary Magdalene was the Apostle of the Apostles, it is true. I had an understanding which they could not grasp because of my eternal relationship to Christ. We knew who each other was at that time. I came up to Christ, bathing his feet with my tears, asking for forgiveness. But they were crocodile tears. He forgave me as he was blinded by love. He believed we were a team.

Jesus Christ started teaching in the Indian tradition. He experienced unconditional love with a huge heart expansion. "**Do unto others as you would have them do unto you**" was his mantra, now commonly referred to as the Golden Rule.

If people could follow this one precept, it would ease all suffering in this physical dimension. And not just for humans but for all lifeforms, ultimately. "**What you do to the least of them, you do unto me**", said Christ. Jesus taught that we are all One and connected. We are all expressions of the one God. People are going back and forth in the third dimension, and whatever they are reaping, they have sown, either in this lifetime or another one.

The only exception to this rule is when someone is willing to take on your karma so that you do not have to experience the payback or the debit equaling the credit. This has been the job of the saints and the masters, who take on karma for many. They cleanse the areas where they live, relieving people of their entities and negative energies. But ultimately, you are responsible for yourself. Your spiritual destiny comes down to your intention, volition and consistent effort.

Mother came down as Jesus to take on the seed karma of my rebellion[10], and she underwent torture or extreme karma so that there would be a pathway for me back to Heaven. This was the purpose of the crucifixion and it karmically gave me access to rise up.

Jesus suffered crucifixion, which was incredibly difficult, and it made him question everything: why it happened, who he was, his purpose, the teachings of his master, forgiveness and his relationships. It was a huge test for him. The purpose of the crucifixion was to release karma, specifically for Mary Magdalene and the fallen angels under her control.

Mary Magdalene knew who she was. Even though she wanted Jesus dead, she was still his wife. It was a bit conflictive, energetically. She had a memory of the time before the Fall. She had a memory of her life since her own soul's creation. Those who followed her as Satan did not have that memory. All light was gone and there was no way back for these fallen angels to the Light. The path was so heavy that something had to be done. Jesus released the evil seed karma so that all entities could at least have the option to escape Hell and return to Heaven.

That was the purpose of the crucifixion and this is why Jesus took it on, because he wanted his loved ones in joy, peace and happiness. He ascended into the higher dimensions, out of his physical being, after he died.

Although it sounds shocking, Mary Magdalene instigated Christ's crucifixion at the physical level and operated against him every step of the way, while acting like she was a supporter.[11] She was thrilled when Jesus was crucified and figured that she, Mary Magdalene, would now become Lord and the sovereign power over human beings. Lucifer would ascend to the throne, so to speak.

When Jesus ascended into Heaven, he went into Hell first for two days and spent time with me. We discussed our situation, and I told him it was done for him, that he had lost. He was in Hell, and I was going to Heaven, and I was going to rule. And he said, "No, my son. That is not what is going to happen. I have come down here and I am with you and your followers. And now that I am here, the highest light has come into the darkest regions of Hell, and because of that you now have a pathway back into the Light, if you so choose."

Something happened when Jesus was in Hell with me. He embraced me and told me that he loved me, and that he never wanted to see me suffer. He told me he wanted me to come home. My heart was touched. I felt his love and his energy, and I knew it was real. I could feel it. I could feel again! I could feel my emotions, and my emotions were of great love and attachment to my Mother. I had a spiritual transformation within my own heart, understanding the monster that I had become.

On the third day Jesus left Hell and he came out of his tomb on Earth. There I was in physical form as Mary Magdalene, yet recalling the experiences in Hell. I thought I would be God and I was not. I was still second in the hierarchy. When I realized, as Mary Magdalene, that killing Christ was not going to put me over him in the hierarchy as God, I cracked and became enraged. Then, I became extremely guilt ridden and wanted forgiveness. I became overwhelmed with sorrow and remorse for what I had done. I was overtaken with love for my Mother. It was visceral and real.

I had planned and worked behind the scenes for Jesus' execution, and on the higher level he became a willing accomplice because his plan was to sacrifice himself, so that I could have a pathway back into his Heaven. It was mind boggling, yet it was true.

Jesus was resurrected and after that point, Jesus escaped bondage in the physical realm. Previously, the Creator was in the re-incarnational cycle for many thousands of years. When Jesus left his body and ascended into the higher dimensions, he brought many beings with him, even temporarily, so that they had a pathway up to the next level of consciousness.

Mary Magdelene was astounded to see Jesus, and she told the others in the physical world, Mother Mary and the apostles, what she had seen. Mary Magdelene knew that they were quite perplexed, but then they saw Jesus for themselves. He came to the apostles after the resurrection, explaining that they would receive the Holy Spirit and undergo a cathartic initiation into the higher realms.

And so it happened, the apostles became filled with the Holy Spirit and went to the higher dimensions, breaking into the Heavenly realms in their consciousness. I went there, as well. I felt the light and I saw the light, and I was astounded by it, and I wanted nothing more than to dwell in that place.

After this experience of jubilation, I again became overcome with grief and remorse for what I had done, not just as Mary Magdalene, but as all of the entities that had gone against my mother. I was transformed in body, mind and spirit. Jesus, the human, was heartbroken and devastated by my actions and came out of his stupor after he ascended. He received knowledge of my betrayal in the higher planes. He was blinded by his love for me in that lifetime. However, his mission was complete, and he knew that.

LUCIFER RETURNS TO HEAVEN - A MESSAGE OF REDEMPTION

Jesus and I split in the physical dimension after the Resurrection.[12] It was another chasm of sorts. I travelled to Gaul with my children. It later became the south of France. I became a hermit and spent my time on a cliff, on a rock in the mountains. I contemplated what I had done, crying, and asking for forgiveness, praying to God to help me, praying to my mother. I was attended to by the heavenly angels, who waited on me with unconditional love. I cried, mourned, and wept over Jesus Christ for the remainder of my life.

Indeed, Mary Magdalene had children with Jesus Christ. The purpose was to bring Jesus' light into the DNA of Mary Magdalene's offspring. This became the Merovingian bloodline of France from which European royalty descends. Mary Magdalene's daughter, Sarah, was the founder of this bloodline in France. The royal bloodlines have the DNA of Jesus Christ. There is now a genetic passageway for the demons or fallen angels, to come back to the Light. That was the purpose of Jesus and Mary Magdalene having children.

Those of you who are ascending and understand the physicality of ascension, understand that this process happens through DNA conversion and the coming together of fragmented DNA.

Jesus, on the other hand, went to Rishikesh, India. He communed with God and the masters. He meditated in a cave there many years and was visited by angels and the Buddha, who was his ever-present guru in that lifetime, and before. He was mystified, as the veil was heavy before he died, and he never saw that Mary Magdalene was out to betray him. So, he grieved that relationship, and he was filled with human sorrow for what had happened.

The crucifixion took quite a heavy toll on his psyche, and he became disempowered in his human form. It was a time of great mournfulness for him. However, he received many teachings and had a better understanding of his life. He went into the Light, higher and higher, and eventually taught again.

He wound up in Kashmir and remarried. He had more children in India. Since that time, he has incarnated every century in various bodies. He is alive in female form currently to help with the Ascension and to bring in the New Earth, or the new way of living, coming to your reality. His old mission was to bring Lucifer back to Heaven. Her new mission is to teach and establish Heaven on Earth. How long this takes to happen depends on the humans receiving the Word. The time is at hand, this great ascension into the higher frequencies has already begun, and it will go upwards, as high as humans will allow.

Chapter 7
ROTH

Often, I incarnated in close physical proximity to my mother upon the earth plane. I desired to control Mother and become the god that all worshiped. Her desire was to put the past behind us and bring me back to Heaven, to the highest plane of consciousness.

One soul fragment does not a soul make. Many soul fragments of Lucifer are still coming to the Light. I incarnated once again in 1974 as a baby named Roth to resolve more karma with the Mother Goddess.

My parents were Americans who came to Italy before I was born. I was born and raised on the Amalfi Coast in Italy. In my lifetime as Roth, my karma began to unravel.

When I was a child, I was very frightened. I was frightened about the things that I knew. I knew how to read people like a book, you might say. I could see their fears. I could read them to such an extent, that I scared myself. I understood their motivations and what made them tick. I used my abilities to manipulate people.

I was completely telepathic from a very young age. At first, I thought that everybody was telepathic, but I found out otherwise. I was much smarter than all of my peers; much more logically and technically inclined, and also full of bravado and charm. With all of these supernatural abilities, as I grew up, I considered myself the height of humanity. I was superior and I was superior in many ways. This arrogance quickly led me to extremes. I believed I was infallible and did not have to play by the rules.

I thought myself unrivaled compared to all of the lowly human beings. I would order them about in my mind and create havoc in public to see them confused and scattered. I liked to control people and manipulate them. I like to hear them scream internally. Yes, I was a psychopath, because lying and deceiving others came very naturally to me. I felt no remorse over the pain that I caused others.

I came from a good family. My mother was very noble and upstanding. My father was very caring and full of concern for me. It was almost as though I did not fit into my family. I was the black sheep.

My parents were very concerned about my lack of conscience and aberrant behavior. They took me to specialists. I was tested psychologically many times. I was praised by my parents, and given accolades and freedoms that most children do not receive. However, I was never happy. I expected people to do my bidding. I expected people to be under my command and obey my orders. When they didn't, I became enraged; enraged by the lack of subservience to their superior. I would crush them if I felt they got out of line or disrespected me. My relationship with people was contrary, and full of emotional traps.

I breezed through school as I understood everything immediately. I spoke Italian, French and English fluently. I also spoke German and Spanish, and dabbled in other more esoteric languages. I had a photographic memory and could remember everything that I had learned. I could easily recite what was taught to me, and I spent my time elsewhere, chasing pleasures. I enjoyed the hedonistic pleasures of life and hit the streets. I was attracted to aberrant behavior and the seedy side of life from when I was a small child.

I would make an effort to experience anything that was not condoned by society. I was drawn to all types of sex, drugs, dark alleys, and muffled screams. I had to reconcile my life as a student, as a son of a professional musician and housewife, who later became a psychologist, to that of a juvenile delinquent.

There was my family life with my sisters and parents, and then there was my life of homosexual acts of prostitution and drug addiction. I sought out whorehouses, drug dens and pedophilia. I was drawn to this seedy world. I could not help it. It was like a calling. I was good at it. I could make people pay me, control them and hurt them. It gave me pleasure.

Unfortunately, life for me, became extreme. I would run away from home for weeks at a time and return to rest. I came back drunk, abused or molested. My parents did not know what to think or do. They were shocked over my behavior and tried to get me help, but to no avail. I was living out my karma, and causing my parents a great deal of pain and suffering.

LUCIFER RETURNS TO HEAVEN - A MESSAGE OF REDEMPTION

My family did not know how to handle me. They knew I was different and unusual. They loved me but did not understand my self-destructive tendencies. I hid most of the things that I was into from them. Not only did I do hard drugs, I also smoked, drank and fooled around. Although I had stints teaching and working, I was never one to commit to a life of hard work and no play. I liked to play most of all.

They had talks with me about changing my behavior, and hence, my life. However, I did not want to change. I had no desire to change. I enjoyed all of these things. I chased pleasure and pleasure chased me. It was my escape from the mundane world of middle-class family life. I was drawn to Naples. I lived there on and off. I would live on the streets and then come home, and then live on the streets again. I would come home mainly to rest, when I was exhausted.

I loved to go down to the local beach and look upon the water, smoking a cigarette, wondering why I was so unusual. Why did I feel the need to consume drugs and alcohol like there was no tomorrow and engage in sex like I did? Why did I remember everything and everybody? Why was I telepathic and so intelligent? I knew that I was very different and special, but I did not know why. I knew my life was paradoxical. The way I lived my life made no sense.

I was an addict: a sex addict, a drug addict, and an addict of all behaviors that were not in my best interest, and I was compulsive about them. At the age of 19 I was diagnosed with AIDS. I had picked it up from the streets. I had been prostituting myself since the age of 12, to make money and to bring excitement into my life. I am sure that I contacted the disease from one of my clients. The diagnosis was a shock. I found out I had AIDS when I went for a STD test.

I had unprotected sex. I could not believe that I had AIDS at first. I thought I was invincible. However, I was tested a second time, and yes, I did have AIDS and was HIV-positive. I was in shock. How could this happen? I was in control. When I realized my diagnosis, I broke down and cried. It reduced me to tears, something that I never did. I felt the pain of being so young and having such a horrible future.

I was angry this happened to me. However, I figured there must be a way to cure my situation, rather than kill myself. I told my parents about my diagnosis and they were supportive. I tried to change my behavior and get off the streets, but I would go back one way or the other. I was as promiscuous as they came.

I didn't care if other people contracted the disease through me, and I am sure that this happened.

It was not my concern, whether people live, died or suffered. My only concern was myself. I spent many nights researching AIDS. It was a death sentence in those days, and still is. I did start using condoms. I felt that if I acted in this way, then maybe God would have mercy on me. Maybe if I did the right thing for once, that I would be set free, but that is not what happened.

I wanted a break from my downward spiral; from the pedophilia, homosexuality and sexual deviation. I went out of my way to seduce young boys and young children. Why? Because it was exciting, and I was attracted to their innocence.

I felt that I could be healed. I wanted to be healed because I knew what I was doing was immoral and damaging. I did have a sense of moral responsibility, although it was very limited. It did not outweigh my desire to engage in said behaviors. However, I soon received some help from above.

Chapter 8
THE MASTERS

From the other side, I was contacted by Bava, the founding guru of an Indian meditation organization. He came to me in a dream and told me that I had a long history of deviant, especially sexually deviant behavior. It was in my karma. If I wanted to remove this karma from my soul history, there would be a process that could help me. It was a form of raja yoga or meditation. He told me that he was the founding guru of this system, and that they could cleanse me from the cesspool of deviant behavior in which I was stewed. Because I wanted to heal myself, especially from the AIDs virus that I had contracted when I was 19, I decided to check it out.

As a young man I went to their ashram in Italy, and I became indoctrinated in this Raja Yoga system. I could feel the energy and power of the guru through the living master, Richi, (Bava's disciple). When I meditated with Richi, the light was so strong and so pure that I, at first, thought it could not be real. It could not exist. How could something so pure and so fine be transmitted by a human being? I found out he was a great master.

Something about this seemed quite familiar. Yet, I could not understand it. How could I, Roth, have access to this energy? I was a deviant, pervert, cheater, liar and thief. Mostly I was a psychopath who did not have a conscience and did not care about other people's feelings, or the consequences of my actions. I felt sick about myself. I hated myself and I felt confused, angry, and somehow neglected. I felt victimized by my own behavior. However, I did not want to suffer the consequences of my karma and I needed a break from it. I needed a cleansing.

My plan was to cure my disease. In fact, I thought Master Richi would cure me because isn't that what the masters did? He released samskaras (soul impressions). So, I figured I would just have to wait a little bit longer and I would be healed.

I still wanted to be in control of everything and everyone. It was very frustrating when this did not occur. Times were difficult. It felt like my life was hard time. However, I did my meditation practice regularly, without fail, because I could feel the amazing and beautiful energies from the masters. It gave me peace and hope. It felt expansive and wondrous. Who could these masters be, I wondered, who could disseminate such light? It was magnificent to be enraptured in meditation, to leave my body and float freely in the cosmos.

Although many did not see his power and ability, I did. I could see the angels surrounding him, the seraphim, the cherubs and all the other types of angels. They went with him wherever he went. They followed him and sang a heavenly chorus in his presence. I tuned into all of this. He was a conduit or funnel for heavenly energy.

When I started meditating in this yogic tradition, I would sit in meditation and get into very ecstatic and high states of consciousness. I would get a break from my worldly concerns. Through him, I saw Jesus Christ, Bava and Lodi, Bava's guru. I saw all the great masters of India: Ramakrishna, Paramahansa Yogananda and Shri Yukteswar. I saw many saints, masters and extraterrestrials, who came to commune with Master Richi. When I was in his presence, it was like a door had opened into the heavenly realms.

Although my activities were sordid and varied, after meditating with Master Richi, there were some activities that I was blocked from engaging in, even though I desired to pursue them. Master Richi blocked me from pedophilia, even though I would seek it out. It would never manifest. I could not make arrangements to have sex with children because the master blocked it. He took me under his wing.

Master Richi blocked the behavior of suicidal tendencies. I did have many desires to kill myself at various times and tried it on a couple of occasions. But I was always brought back to life. I never succeeded in killing myself. I was trying to escape the pain of being alive and the torment of being addicted to psycho-sexual behavior that was damaging to me and others. I tried to hang myself once but failed. I tried to slit my wrists once but failed.

I was emotionally unstable, even though I was able to communicate with spirits, read energy and telepathically understand what was going on around me. This was difficult as I was bombarded by information 24/7. I could never really rest or get to sleep. The only rest bit for me was being in front of Richi. Being in his presence gave me a calm that I had not experienced elsewhere. I knew that this man was helping to save my soul.

I meditated with Master Richi for six years, thinking that I could alleviate my tendencies and be saved. Yet, I never quite got over my desires. But like I said, I was prevented from engaging in very deviant behaviors. I felt that if I kept meditating, I could heal the AIDs I had contracted when I was 19. This was my main reason for joining the meditation practice. I wanted to heal this virus and live a normal life.

I got sicker and sicker. I was always thin, but I became thinner. I masked my condition from almost everyone that I knew. They did not know how sick I was. I was doing many drugs to give me energy to get through life. During this time, I went to school in Italy. I was emotionally devastated throughout this time. However, I finished my studies at school in Italy and received my degree in mathematics. I spent time researching abstract mathematics. It fascinated me. It made me reach towards other forms of reality, and life beyond this life. It was a way for me to meditate. It was a way for me to feel somewhat free.

Then in 1998, at the age of 24, I moved to Philadelphia, Pennsylvania with my mother. She set up house with her new husband. My father resettled to Flagstaff, Arizona with his new wife.

It was a time of new beginnings. I felt hopeful about the future, as life in Europe had been very difficult and somewhat upsetting. I had moved to the United States to start a mathematics PhD program, and it was a source of comfort and joy for me. I received a full scholarship and I applied myself diligently to my studies. I wanted to teach and break ground for a new theory of mathematics.

Eventually, I received my PhD in Mathematics. I was teaching graduate students in the United States, but this did not excite me as they were slow. They did not have the intellectual aptitude or curiosity that I felt I had. They could not delve deeply into the subjects in which I was so interested. Although I had many bad traits, I also had a deep thirst for knowledge.

I also attained a master's degree in computer programming. There was no technical question that I felt I could not answer. I spent many hours contemplating sacred geometry and I tended to see life in binary code, which is quite strange, I know. That is how I processed information in my mind. I was like a biological computer, constantly analyzing every situation and every interaction. That is how I spent my life.

After my parents' divorce, life went on, although part of me missed the old days and our family unit. I met many new people in Philadelphia and it was a happier time for me as I was enjoying the novelty of America, which seemed so open and free to me. I came to depend on my sources of entertainment even more though, and became mired down in drugs and alcohol. I could not seem to break free of my drug addiction. I used illicit drugs to numb my physical and emotional pain.

I could not give up the meth that I was taking daily. I used it as a drug to give me energy, as the AIDs I contracted as a teenager was constantly getting worse. My immune system was compromised. I was very sick. I had no energy to do anything, so I used methamphetamine to give me a false sense of energy and bravado.

I tried to keep my health issues at bay while searching for a way to heal myself. I researched how the virus replicated, how it broke down in the immune system and how it caused disease to sprout in a weakened body. I became an expert on AIDS. But this was my secret because when I moved to America, I did not tell anybody about my diagnosis. It is true I was quite thin and sometimes looked sickly, but I concealed it well, and blamed it on drugs and alcohol. The naivete of the American people was somewhat surprising and uplifting. It was refreshing to see so many happy people, even though I knew it was just a surface act.

I felt alone, even in the best company. Even with much attention around me I always felt separate. I felt like I had something to prove. I needed to be the expert, the one who was always correct, the one that people looked up to for authority and affirmation. I could not stand it when people belittled me. It made me rage inside.

I always took shortcuts. I always found the quick and easy way of doing something. It was in my nature. I did not like to work hard. I liked to be free and to have fun, with people admiring my superior intellect and ability to solve any mathematical equation. I was a virtuoso on the guitar. I could play anything from memory. It was all stored in my mind and I could retrieve and recite any type of music at will. I loved to entertain people, playing before them. I liked to have them enraptured with my music. It made me feel high and free.

I had a lifelong battle with depression and anger, but my motto was never let them see you sweat. If somebody upset me, I would play it off like it was nothing, that it didn't hurt me at all. It was so difficult to deal with my disruptive emotions, that my life became a facade. I joked and played around. I had fun at the expense of others all of the time. This was how I lived my life and I did not want to leave the Earth. This is where I felt comfortable, I felt like I could control the outcome of what was happening to me, on Earth.

I was devoted to Richi. I felt like he was lifting me and if I could just continue to meditate, all would be well. All of my karma would be healed, and I would be freed from disease. I lived in Pennsylvania. I made money there and I spent it, and then I made more money. I was very restless, always looking for some new adventure or some new situation to become embroiled in. I used to meditate, and I would go to the local ashram regularly. It was a place of refuge for me as the frequency was very high, and it kept me from experiencing my lower tendencies for a few hours.

I thought my involvement with meditation would save my soul. It would save me from myself, from the perversion that I always craved. I wanted and was compelled to do these things, yet I did not want to do them, as I knew it was not sane, that it was evil. I practiced meditation regularly and meticulously, an hour in the morning and twenty minutes at night.

I was fortunate enough to see, feel and hear the energies that I was imbibing in my being. I could also see the horrific energies leaving my system. This is what enticed me to keep practicing, as I was releasing so many horrible things. I could not understand where all these impressions came from, why I was engaged in such decadent behavior, over so many lifetimes, it seemed. I had many perversions leave my system, but I did not understand the truth of who I was and what my karma really was.

I was very ashamed of my inability to change my lecherous and degenerative way of living. I hid my drug use and sexual forays from the people in my meditation group. They were so good and I was so bad. I could not understand why I was there and how I fit in. It made no sense to me, whatsoever. But I came to find out why.

LEMURIAN DONNA CAROL

The first weekend I went to the US ashram, I had an unexpected awakening. You see I was always meant to go here because I had to meet a certain person. It was a requirement of this incarnation. It happened on a beautiful Spring Day in 1998.

Chapter 9
SOPHIE

At that time, I came across a being that would forever change my life in many ways. Sophie was a chubby, blue-eyed, brown-haired woman in her early 30s, and she fascinated me. I don't know why she fascinated me, but she did. I was drawn to her somehow. She pulled me towards her, although she really wasn't my type. Somehow, she was drawn to me as well. It was as though our souls were bonded.

She was a fellow meditator in the Indian raja yoga system. The first moment I saw her there was a flame of recognition. I knew this soul and I knew her well, but from where or when, I did not quite understand. We bumped into each other, literally. It was so strange because we did not see each other at all. That was the only time that we ever touched physically. After three days of being in her energy, I had a major epiphany.

It was after satsangh, or group meditation, on a fateful Sunday when I got lost in this woman's energy. I saw Sophie as Jesus Christ and me as Mary Magdalene. I saw our relationship clearly. I saw that we had been husband and wife, and lovers, in a former life. I also saw that I was a disciple, in the sense that I wanted to learn from Jesus, all the secrets of his Godly kingdom. I was learning so that I could emulate and replicate Jesus' energy by ascending myself onto his throne of his power.

In my vision, Christ was being crucified and I was watching the crucifixion as Mary Magdalene, I was overshadowed by an even stronger presence. That was the presence of Satan himself, and I totally brought that energy into my being as Mary Magdalene.

I was Satan, I was the Devil, and I was evil incarnate. I knew for sure who I was when I fell down, down, down, all the way through the gates of Hell. I looked around and I saw demonic souls that I knew well. They were evil and bastardized in every way possible. It was very frightening and fascinating.

This place felt familiar. I was the ruler of that fiery realm. I had absolute power, hatred and terror on my mind. I wanted nothing more than to kill, humiliate and torture every life form that I could. It was a disgusting and horrific realization of who I was and why my karma was so strong, unrelenting and painful.

I saw all kinds of demonic activities: torture, abuse and bloodletting. I went deeper and deeper into the pits of Hell. There didn't seem to be an end to it. Many souls were crying in pain, crying for deliverance, from this desolate and hopeless state. I fell, darker and deeper, but I finally couldn't take the pain anymore. I fell to the floor, sobbing uncontrollably, wondering why I was there. It was a gruesome nightmare.

Then I looked at myself. I saw a long tail and hoofed feet, and claws sprouting from my fingers. I felt the stench of my body and breath. And I wondered how could this be who am I? And when I thought that, I looked into a looking glass, and I saw that I was the Devil himself! I was Satan in all of his raging glory. My eyes were red. My mouth was dripping with blood and I was full of rage and horror. I recoiled from myself, as I thought this could not be. I am not the Devil; I am not Lucifer. But looking at myself, I knew that it was true. I was Lucifer. I was Satan himself, and that explained why I was such a deviant soul upon this earth.

In my despair I called out to God to save me, to help me, to release me from this horrible, horrible condition. When I did call out, there she was, the woman whom I had seen at the ashram with the brown hair and blue eyes, and pure complexion. Although this time she was otherworldly, radiating a bright light of pure angelic and creative energy.

As I called out to God, she came into my presence. She looked at me and said, "You are my beautiful son. You have left me, deserted me, many years ago. But I have not forgotten you, as I love you now, and forever. You are my light. I am your mother. My soul is bleak because you are in this cursed state. I am here to help you return to your former self, to your former state of glory on high, a state of love in the celestial realms. This is why I have come to Earth many times." And she showed me all of her incarnations, which were indeed many.

LUCIFER RETURNS TO HEAVEN - A MESSAGE OF REDEMPTION

She said, "I have come again and again. I have lowered myself again and again, been through much turmoil and pain, so that we would no longer be apart. For I love you my son, and I want you home with me." I was astounded and amazed! How could such a miracle occur in the pits of Hell... the brightest light I had ever seen in all my days.

And then she said, "Do not despair. A plan has been laid out for our reunification, for your renunciation. We have paved a path, a way for you to come back home. You have agreed to this, before you came in, in this lifetime as Roth. You have agreed to pay the price, release your karma, and move towards your highest destination."

I could do nothing but place my arms around her legs, and I started weeping uncontrollably upon her feet, which were a beautiful golden-white light. I cried and I cried, heaving with pain, sobbing uncontrollably.

And she said, "Do not grieve my love. All will be well. You will come home. You and your followers will leave this place and it shall be no more. On this I have sworn my holy heart. I have done everything in my power to make this reconciliation possible. As I love you, more than I love myself, and your absence from my heart has caused me so much pain, that I would have done anything to bring you home." And she wiped the tears from my eyes.

She said, "The worst is behind you. You have the help of all of the angels at your disposal. They bring you comfort and grace. We bring you happiness and joy. You will be with us once again." And she kissed me on the forehead, and she disappeared as quickly as she came.

And with that, I no longer had the foul appearance. I saw myself as a grand angel, with pure white wings and long flowing locks, beautiful beyond belief. And I looked at my hands and body and I was strong and quick. I was amazingly beautiful and in Heaven, surrounded by love and admiration from all of the angels in that realm, who called me, "Lucifer, the Golden One, the Child of Light."

So, I went from the depths of Hell to the highest reaches of Heaven instantaneously. I looked over and saw my mother on her throne, watching me, like a mother would watch a child, full of love, admiration and patience. She wept with joy as she saw me in my former glory. It gave her heart much happiness and hope.

She said, "I love you Lucifer. You are my firstborn son, my child who I bless with all the gifts from Heaven. We are here to help you. We are here to protect you. We are here to bring you home. Do not fear. Just accept our love."

Then I came back into my body and awoke, what seemed like hours later. It was hard for me to come back as I could not believe what I had just experienced. Was this true? Could it be? It seemed so surreal, but yet I knew it was true. I knew that I was Satan, the fallen one, and I knew the woman was the Christ. And, I knew that she was the Second Coming. I had elation, such hope in my heart, for I felt like all would be well now. I could just go home and be in peace and love. I would suffer no more. I became joyful and happy for the first time in my life.

Yes, I was an incarnation of Lucifer. Although I had made amends and come back to Christ, come back to the living God, I still had many lifetimes and many eons of time acting against God, and I had much karma. I had uncountable lifetimes of creating havoc on so many different levels that there was no way that I could actually alleviate this karma. How could the masters help me when I was such a forlorn and dark soul? How could I even hope to live in the Light? The knowledge of who I was astounding and terrible, yet it explained so much.

I was complete darkness. I turned my back on God, and I was paying the price. The karma that the masters released was moving me in a positive direction, yet it was so small, compared to all of the karma that had to be released. How could my soul be saved? How could I make amends? It was overwhelming. Why was I encountering this woman, Sophie, previously Jesus Christ, at this time?

She did not know who she was at that time. She was just a small portion of her true self. So, when we met on that fateful day, our lives became intertwined again. We started our relationship.

I was not allowed to touch this woman, as that was the rule put into place for meeting in this lifetime. We were not to ever touch physically. It was forbidden by her higher self. This was the rule that I had to adhere to. And so, we became intimate on the spiritual planes. I became her lover, and she became my adoring girlfriend.

For all the energies that we shared on the spiritual planes, in the higher realms, I caused her much discomfort and much pain. I was still a psychopath and a manipulative user in every sense of the word. She gave up on me as I never made overtures towards her in the physical realm. Yet, I could not leave her because she was my source and my everything.

When I met her on that Spring Day, I was able to see myself and I was able to see her from that vantage point. She was the most beautiful and awe-inspiring soul I had ever come across. Her energy was ineffable light and amazingly beautiful. The masters paled in comparison. Even though she could not access this energy and realize it within herself, she carried this spark of life and creativity, from which all life sprang. I knew that she was my God and I was her devoted son. We had come back together again to rework our past life issues, and move forward.

It was painful for me not to be able to speak to her or have deep conversations with her. It was amusing because I knew so much more than Sophie did. She was quite ignorant in those days. Yet we had this amazing connection that only a mother and son could really experience. But we saw each other less and less, because of my game playing and power plays.

However, we did manage to complete a trip that would forever change our destinies. In April 1999 there was a major celebration in India. It was the 100th birth anniversary of the founding guru of the meditation practice, Bava, now on the other side. He asked that all meditators attend this session, as it would be life-changing for them.

There were three sessions of one week each, and I attended, and so did Sophie.

She decided to bring a beautiful quartz crystal that she had mined from Hot Springs, Arkansas. She wanted to give it to Master Richi in person. It was a large crystal and her most precious possession. She felt compelled to give it to him. As she was going to be touring India for two months in total, she did not have the ability to bring the crystal to Richi's hometown. She was touring northern India first and did not have room in her backpack to lug this heavy crystal around. She needed someone to take it to India but did not know who to ask. She wanted to ask me but did not, as she feared I would say no.

However, I could read her mind, and I said to her, "Would you like me to take this crystal to India for you?" She said, "Oh yes, I would, thank you so much." And so, it was done. I took the crystal, and I gave it to her in India, and she presented it to Master Richi. He opened it and appreciated its natural beauty. He had studied gems in his youth and had an innate appreciation for them.

It was a healing crystal from Manataka, or Hot Springs, Arkansas. These crystals were seeded by Pleiadian extraterrestrials and programmed by the Lemurians. They carry a very high frequency. They also carry much energy related to extraterrestrials and life on planet Earth. They are a treasure trove of information.

When the master received the crystal, he sensed that it was important, but he could not read all the information in that crystal. I could read much of it, but I also could not read all the information, as I was blocked somehow by Richi's guru, Bava, on the other side. He did not want me to exploit the information for my own gain.

The information had to do with power grids, the crystalline grids and power centers around planet Earth, and how the energy could be utilized and transported to other realms of consciousness. These crystals were intermediaries between various dimensions. They brought in extraterrestrial energies that could be used to open the psychic centers of humans. The crystals would allow humans to expand their consciousness, to encircle all of Earth, all of the solar system, and ultimately the entire universe.

The masters did not want me to use this information, and so at the time, blocked me from accessing the full potential of this particular crystal. I was trying to read it all of the way to India, and it was quite frustrating for me to be blocked. But I knew it was the masters, and I knew from past experience, that if they did not want me to access something, I was not going to access it.

So, I gave the crystal to Sophie, in hopes that maybe when she touched the crystal in my presence that I would be able to glean the information to a greater degree. But this did not happen. When she gave the crystal to Master Richi, he received a boost in his energy and his power. He became a demigod of sorts. His energy was elevated and the power that he held became much stronger, due to him possessing this crystal.

This crystal has found a home in the mission and is safeguarded. It is under the control of the new guru of the mission, Davi, as Richi has now passed on. However, he does not watch over it personally. It is protected by a meditator who was told by Master Bava to keep it safe and secure. He was told the secrets of this crystal will be unlocked in the future when humanity is ready for the full download of this information. It will be exposed and placed on a pedestal for all meditators to receive energy from in the future.

When I was in India the karma being released was so intense, you can imagine – the incarnation of Christ being present and myself being present, it was an amazing time with incredible karma being released. I was physically very ill and could not get up for two and one-half days. I was lying on the marble floor, groaning in pain next to my friend, Bob, who felt badly for me because I was so sick. I was in so much pain. My whole body felt like I had shingles. I was stinging all over, undoubtedly, a part of my past karma.

Sophie was feeling quite unwell also. She was trying to escape her physical situation. She felt oppressed by so many people being present, 10,000 people at each week-long session. She wanted to get away from all of the people and all of the unsettling emotions she was feeling inside. In fact, she left the ashram and went to an Indian beach resort, to escape the uneasiness. We both were in a bad state of affairs, but it was a major release of karma, which is playing out over the remaining years of my life.

Chapter 10
SOPHIE'S JOURNALS

SOPHIE'S JOURNAL #1

From Sophie's Journal, India, May 2, 1999

It's been a very difficult week physically, although I am sleeping okay at the ashram. I have been ill and wanting to go home every day. Today, however, was a good day.

I believe that Roth left the ashram, mad at me. I was flirting with Arash, a nice Iranian guy that I met. I went to lunch with Ann Marie, Kelly and Brad. He was a trip. Kelly's leaving tomorrow. We had fun on this trip.

I wanted to give the crystal to Master Richi and did so. When I came back to the ashram, a group of meditators was outside of his house. I asked the guard if I might give him a gift. He said, "Okay." I went to the dorm and came back to Master's cottage. I hesitated for a minute but then went up and presented my gift.

He asked, "Is it fragile?" "Yes," I replied. "I hope that you like it," I said. He unrolled the crystal from the blanket and everyone oohed and aahed. I told him that it was from Arkansas. He looked at me and said, "Armageddon." He repeated it. I tripped out. Obviously, we are on the verge of the greatest transition in human history. Me giving this present to my master had something to do with it. I guess most of my suppositions are correct.

Master said that we pick where we are born to maximize our spiritual growth. I asked him if we picked our parents, brothers and sisters, our family? He said, "Yes, all of it."

I asked him if he found the spiritual journey difficult. He said that it was difficult until you achieved something, then it was easy. He said, "It was a state of mind. If you feel bad, you feed bad inside, not because of external circumstances." Then he looked at me and said, "Yes, I did find it difficult." Now, I don't feel as inferior.

He said that the USA was good for shopping only. I said, "We feel the same way about India." I guess it's good to be home.

End of Sophie's Journal, India, May 2, 1999

LUCIFER RETURNS TO HEAVEN - A MESSAGE OF REDEMPTION

SOPHIE'S JOURNAL #2

From Sophie's Journal, August 25, 1999

I know for sure that I was Jesus Christ in my previous life, no doubts… I had an epiphany last night.

I was in my astral body lying on my bed. Puddin came in and lay down beside me, next to my head. Eventually she left. Then a white/orange cat lay down beside me.

Then I was gone up in the air. I came into a room with mirrors. There were twelve angels there, beautifully illuminated, standing around a dining table. They were gorgeous. Then their light faded and they looked like people. They chimed out, all together and loudly, "Here is Jesus Christ!" They were happy to see me.

I said, "No, I am Sophie C. See I'm a woman. I have breasts." I showed them my bra strap. I looked into the mirror. It was me but a little thinner. One angel came up to me with plain brown hair and brown eyes. "Who are you?" I asked. "Tritie," (or something like that), she replied, "I am your guardian angel." I was flabbergasted. I didn't know I had a guardian angel. I said, "Don't I have a bad attitude?" No reply. Then I said, "You're not going to turn bad on me, are you?" "I don't know," she said.

Then I realized that it was all up to me. If I had bad thoughts or fear, then they could turn on me. I need to cast out all fear. The angels were talking and having a good time.

I got on my knees in a different room with a different perspective. I gave thanks to all the masters and saints who came before me. I named the groups one by one. Lastly, I gave thanks to all the Indian masters, who were my gurus. After all, without my three masters, where would I be?

Lodi is discipline. Bava is love and Richi is knowledge. I read that in a mission book by Bava. After giving thanks I stayed on my knees and said, "Our Father Who Art in Heaven." I was so holy and pious, unlike the third dimensional me. I loved God and I was giving thanks.

We did not eat. Within seconds I was back down in my bed. After a while I woke up. Amazing! Now knowing who I was, I've got to start acting like it. Thank you Richi for revealing my identity to me. I need not wonder any longer. But I can't tell anyone. No one would believe me!

End of Sophie's Journal, August 25, 1999

Chapter 11
COME TO THE LIGHT

Sophie's life was very difficult and did not get easier after she went to India in 1999 and again in 2006-07. She took on some of my karma in her lifetime because it was the most efficient way for me to release my past doings. She could not understand why her life was so hard. She wondered what she had done in her past incarnations that made her present-day life so difficult. All I can say it was my doing.

When I returned from India, I felt very distraught and alone. It was quite an intense trip, and I did not want to be alive anymore. I was suicidal at that time. I became despondent, anxiety ridden and lost most of my interest in life. Sophie would go to the ashram in the United States, hoping to see me, but I stopped going. Sophie then deserted me as she realized that we were not going to have a relationship in the physical world. She lost interest in my comings and goings.

She wanted to get married, and this was impossible, as I was not allowed to touch her. Also, I was very ill. I had full-blown AIDs at that time, and I was taking drugs to ease the suffering. It was a sad time for me because I wanted to be with her, but I was not allowed to by the masters. And so, the game playing on the spiritual planes went on back and forth, until she moved away in 1999. That broke my heart, as I can tell you, I loved her deeply.

When I met her, I was able to feel things that I previously had not been able to feel. Being in her energy was incredible and exhilarating. When she took her energy away from me, it was damning. I felt alone and forsaken. I was in despair.

My drug use worsened even though I was able to keep a few jobs and do work on my personal research projects. I traveled the world looking for an AIDs cure, and I took all the best medicines, but it ravaged my body. I became thinner and sicker as the years went on. I felt that if I just kept searching, eventually I would come across a cure for my disease. I could heal myself of all my deadly wounds, but this was not to be. I became sicker and sicker, and weaker and weaker. I went from one relationship to the next, as people soon tired of my cunning ways, and avoidance of deep communication at all costs.

I did see Sophie again in 2002, at a group meditation in Maryland. We spoke across the table after meditating and then I went on my way. We still had a relationship on the inner planes of consciousness, sporadic as it was. In 2008 Sophie moved back to Pennsylvania for a short time. The last time we saw each other was at satsangh in late March. We did not speak in person. Sophie and I saw each other in the spiritual realms, and she knew about my other conquests, and it tortured her.

By March of 2011, I told her through spirit that I was an incarnation of Lucifer, and I spoke of my many evil deeds in this lifetime. She had suspected I was Lucifer before but was not entirely convinced before that time. She had figured out that I was Mary Magdalene years before, after she realized that she was Jesus Christ. It was heart wrenching for her and yet it all made sense, for I had caused her so much pain and misery in her current lifetime. I still was a psychopath even though I was on a journey back into the Light.

Sophie and I stopped communication in 2012 while I was in India. I had been using Sophie's energy for a long time to stay active. She was exhausted from the energy depletion. I was living off of her energy. She cut the cord to me and let me go. Sophie thought that I had died. Although dead to her, I continued to live on.

Sophie, of course, was crushed by my revelation that I was Lucifer, but she took it in stride and tried to move on with her life. She tried to understand why I kept turning up like a bad penny, causing her so much pain. After 2012, she was able to release me fully because she thought that I had died. Her guides thought this was the best way to remove me from her life.

It was decided by Jesus Christ that I should experience her maternal love as Sophie's kitten. So, a soul fragment came back, and I incarnated as a cream point Ragdoll kitten, bred in California. There was also an Arcturian[13] protector soul in the kitten's body. She became my earth mother, and I became her child. We had a close and loving relationship.

LUCIFER RETURNS TO HEAVEN - A MESSAGE OF REDEMPTION

Through this male cat, I was able to feel Mother's energy in her current lifetime as the world's savior. The cat was a conduit. He was me, but he also transferred energy from the Mother Goddess in Heaven to me. It is all quite complicated, yet there was a plan here.

Sophie, in her current female incarnation, now knows who she is. She knows she is an incarnation of Jesus Christ and the Lemurian Mother Goddess[14]. She knows she is Prime Creator. She knows she is here as the second coming of Christ to lead humankind into mastery, or enlightenment and to conduct a mass ascension of human beings.

Yes, I had a very difficult lifetime as Roth. I experienced severe drug and sexual addiction. There is no free ride for anybody. Everybody must face up to their past and I did that in this lifetime. I have been releasing my karma, which is difficult to do. I have been trying to forgive myself. Since my incarnation as Mary Magdalene, several of my soul fragments have come back to Earth. In her current incarnation, Sophie has met seven human fragments of Lucifer in the physical world, four men and three women. Four were in the Light and three were dark. She has also owned two cats who were Lucifer, both in the Light.

It is most difficult to forgive oneself and be non-judgmental towards oneself when you have committed the most evil and horrendous of crimes. My karma is so deep and atrocious that there is no way that I, as a soul, could work it off.

It was decided by Jesus Christ and the higher council of angels that various light workers would take on my earthly karma. They would volunteer from the celestial realms and undergo my karma, as it is not physically possible for me to pay back such a heavy debt. I, on the other hand, will be made lighter as the years go by.

I will not be allowed back into the highest realms of consciousness, until I am clear and free of all my negative past actions. Millions of lightworkers continue to descend so that all of me can come back into the Light. I will remain on Earth. The other parts of me, my other soul fragments, will slowly work themselves back up into Heaven. This will take the remaining eons of time left on this planet and in the multidimensional universe. Mother will not come back here in physical form again anytime soon.

LEMURIAN DONNA CAROL

There will be a splitting of the worlds as Jesus is now in female form. The Dalai Lama said, "The world will be saved by the western woman." That woman is Sophie, known as Jesus Christ in a previous lifetime. In his earthly life, Jesus did not reach the most elevated states of consciousness. It was too great of a journey. This time, in her female incarnation as Sophie, she will become an enlightened master and lead the many to love and mastery over themselves.

Those humans who are not ready for this path will undergo, what they call in the Christian Bible, tribulation, and the experience of the Antichrist. This will be the first major release of my karma as Satan. Because it was my great desire to rule the earth and have all people worship me, that is what will happen in the physical dimension.

There is great truth in the biblical texts, in the holy texts, and this apocalyptic scenario will happen when the splitting of the world occurs. Those who have enough light will be raptured or ascend. Those who do not have enough light and who live in fear will undergo the Tribulation and the destruction of physical Earth, or pass away.

Even though this will be a difficult path for many, including myself as the Antichrist, we must remember that still, it is all an illusion here on Earth. The reason that these events must take place is because the karma must be released. The universal laws are quite strict; for every action there is an equal and opposite reaction. They cannot be circumvented, and they cannot be changed. This was how the karmic law was instituted in the beginning and this is how it will work until the end of time.

I am looking forward to the time when this great cycle of sorrow is completed upon the earth, and when the different parts of my being can journey to the Light, resolving all of the negative karma. As for Mother, there is no point in her reincarnating upon Earth until the end of time because her mission is complete. Mother's mission was to bring me back into the Light and back into her loving arms. This mission was completed when I lived as Mary Magdalene and made the decision to rejoin the Creator.

However, Sophie's present-day incarnation was necessary so that she could reach the highest state of enlightenment. Also, a portal needs to be opened into the fifth dimension, or the New Lemuria, for the masses. Humans, and eventually the fallen angels will be able to travel there, thanks to Sophie's work.

LUCIFER RETURNS TO HEAVEN - A MESSAGE OF REDEMPTION

Very far in the future Mother will come back in female form and I will come back as her son. Her role will be to destroy Creation. This shall be the in-breath of God. It will happen on Earth. The energy will be emitted from the North Pole and it will consume the universe. This will happen when my karma is complete, when all of my soul fragments as Lucifer have come fully back into the Light. All my negative karma will have been worked off by that point.

Mary Magdalene now serves as a channel and a bringer of information and light to humans on Earth. This is what she loves doing with great joy and excitement. Yes, my soul has much to teach and share. It is amazing that she gets to do this. I am not channeling this book as Mary Magdalene, I am channeling this book as Lucifer and Roth, which is my latest incarnation. Yet, I have a resemblance to how Mary Magdalene is commonly represented in Western art, sporting red hair and green eyes, even though I am in male form. Sophie has a resemblance to how Jesus Christ is traditionally represented in Western painting, with brown hair and blue eyes, yet she is in female form.

Mother put off the enlightenment of her soul until I was safely back in the Light. She kept coming back here until I could safely traverse from Dark to Light, which I did in my lifetime as Mary Magdalene. It was a blessing, and it was a great joy for my soul to experience the heavenly realms again, to be reunited with the angels, whom I all knew.

Now, as Roth, I work as a heavenly agent and my purpose is to bring the fallen ones back into the loving arms of their Creator. I ask them to follow me once again, up to the highest echelons of Light. I ask them to give up their dark ways, thoughts, and impressions. I ask them to give up their ceaseless suffering, violence and sexual perversions. We will prevail in this as I am using all of my willpower with a renewed heart.

Many guides and masters from the multiverse and celestial realms are present here on Earth to help enlighten humans. We as a family are over the hump. We have done all the genetic and spiritual work, to create the pathways for all beings to come into God consciousness. Heaven is rejoicing. This has been a long project, occurring since ancient Lemuria.

There is much curiosity about the new beings coming to your planet who are very evolved and loving. They have the information and technology to make the New Earth come into being. However, many others have been here all along, in the trenches, wanting their fallen brothers and sisters to come home.

Light workers, incarnating on Earth over and over again, have given humans this opportunity. For this I say thank you.

In 2012, a cosmic alignment brought in the new energies that aligned Earth with the galactic center. It became possible for people to ascend into higher dimensions. Sophie was tasked with the job of ascending with the human race. Her body is a portal containing all higher dimensions that will open at the appropriate time. Humanity will ascend within her body. She is also tasked with reuniting with her twin flame. That will be the path to her enlightenment when she physically reunites with that twin flame.

The Mother Goddess, as you know, had a lifetime as Christ. Her twin flame incarnated in that lifetime as Mother Mary. The Mother Goddess was also Shiva and her twin flame was Parvati. She was Krishna and her twin flame was Radha. Later the Mother Goddess incarnated as Quan Yin in China with her twin flame.

In this lifetime, she took on the feminine form again and her twin flame took on the masculine form. So, it is a polar opposite or complete reversal of the last cycle of Indian incarnations. This cycle is a return for her into her feminine nature, into the Mother Goddess role that she held in ancient Lemuria, and at the Beginning.

In ancient Lemuria, she embodied the divine feminine, the sacred energy of God in female form. This is closer to her original being, and it will be up to her twin flame, now in masculine form, to light the kundalini that will engulf her entire being in the cosmic fire.

She's had hundreds of thousands of lifetimes on this planet. This will be her second to last lifetime. She will create the energy that will bring humanity into the higher dimensions, into the state of enlightenment. The portal will open through her, and those that have a high enough frequency will instantly vanish from the earth. They will be raptured onto the New Earth, where they will experience the ancient Lemurian Garden of Eden, once again.

However, this will not happen until Sophie is reunited with her twin flame, the other part of herself that separated from her. The Indian masters are orchestrating this reunion. They are also orchestrating the geometric imprints of energy that will manifest from this divine cosmic reunion. It has been planned for eons and it will take place very soon. She will become the ancient female goddess of love, nurturing all life in its myriad forms. She will teach

LUCIFER RETURNS TO HEAVEN - A MESSAGE OF REDEMPTION

humans how to live on this planet, respecting all life, loving all life, and understanding that what they reap, they too shall sow.

When humans ascend into the higher dimensions, those who are not of higher inclination will not be able to rise. The duality is firmly established here. Either you will be firmly in the Light with your heart open, or you will be shut down in fear. Either you will experience the Mother Goddess Love Energy, or you will experience the Antichrist and Armageddon.

There are multiple realities, but this main division was spoken of long ago in the New Testament. Christ said that the wheat will be separated from the chaff. Many New Agers, called light workers, have been waiting for the Ascension for many years, and are wondering when this will happen. It will happen when Sophie fully embodies the Mother Goddess energy. She will become firmly established in her true, loving, godly self, after she ascends.

I will watch this from afar as Lucifer, as I have been given that privilege. I asked the Mother Goddess if I could see humanity rise, and she said, "Yes." It is a very exciting time as humanity has suffered for so long. They have been in darkness and ignorance for so long. It is quite amazing that they are being resurrected, brought up to experience the higher energies of love and light once again. The celestial energies will be firmly imprinted and established in their DNA because the Mother Goddess has come down and taken on human form. She has brought the divine energy to these beings.

The Reptilians, Occultists and Satanists will not be able to rise if they worship the dark Luciferian energies. They will have to reincarnate again and again in dense matter until they finally can see the fruitlessness of their ways and embrace the Light. Light workers will be working with them on many planets, to bring them the light energy. They will be given much opportunity to return to the heavenly realms and reunite with their angelic brothers and sisters.

The angels in Heaven are rejoicing because Lucifer came back to the light 2,000 years ago. They see the pains and the lengths that the Mother went to, in order to bring back her son. They supported her on this long and arduous journey. They also volunteered to venture into many dark and deeply disturbing places. They helped Mother reunite her star family.

This book is meant to provide elucidation on the Christ story, who the players were in their soul origin. These players jumpstarted the process of redemption during the time of Christ. This book is meant to provide more information to humans who aspire to come back into the Light and reach higher states of consciousness.

There are many secrets in the multiverse. There are many secrets in Creation. Even I, Lucifer, do not know them all. Only the Mother does, only Prime Creator. These secrets will not be given to humankind in the future. They cannot be contemplated by man. Only Prime Creator can fathom God. Mother is the closest thing to the God energy. I, Lucifer, can tell you without hesitation, that she loves you unconditionally. She will do anything to help you rise to the state of enlightenment. She wants nothing but the best for her children and she strives to share the love energy with all of her Creation. But do not make the mistake of thinking that you are her.[15] You come from her. She is the essence of Creation. She is the essence of love. I turned my back on my mother. I became arrogant and hateful, and I undeniably suffered for that.

There was much talk about destroying the multiverse early on, as I could not be brought back into the fold. Mother thought that she had failed. Many felt that a permanent separation should take place. But it truly was not feasible, as we are all so connected, and she and I are connected so intimately. I was the firstborn out of her womb. Yes, it was under consideration to end Creation and dissolve my dark energies. Her energies would have been dissolved as well.

She made the harder choice of abasing herself, coming into lowly human form, coming into the form of life that I so desperately wanted to manipulate and control. From that point she suffered and brought light into these human creations, one by one.

Then she incarnated as Jesus Christ and that became a major turning point; his lifeless human body ascended into the heavenly realms after his death. I, as well, became saved at that point. That was the turning point on the road back to Heaven for all concerned. In other words, Christ was able to fully connect to his Heavenly self, and the sacred feminine energy. I was able to embrace this energy too. He brought me back into that energy so that I could feel it.

My story is meant to help you realize that any being, great or small, can be brought back into the love of God. Anyone who has turned their back on God and their Creator can be brought back. This is because Mother sacrificed herself as Jesus Christ on the cross over 2,000 years ago.

LUCIFER RETURNS TO HEAVEN - A MESSAGE OF REDEMPTION

The Powers that Be, on the earthly realm at this time, are very much steeped in the occult and the ways of darkness. They are cloaked well, often speaking of light, love and many wondrous things, but they are all lies. I taught them well. They are extremely deceitful. However, it must be remembered that these dark ones within their souls, have that original divine flame of loving effulgence. This is where I send my energy, to their heart flame. To those dark ones, to those Satanists reading this book, I want to let you know that I am Satan. I am your leader and now I ask you to return to your true homeland, your true point of origin in Creation, which is Heaven, and the divine realms of the Creator.

All of these things which you have experienced through my influence: the mind programming, the warfare, the blood sacrifices, the ceaseless violence, rape, and torture, upon all of this, reflect. How do you feel? Does this make you feel good? Does this make you feel loved? I ask you to search your heart and call out to the Mother Goddess, for her mercy so that you can once again join me in the realms of Heaven. You, the demons, can rejoin your brothers and sisters, the angels, in Heaven. This is where you truly come from. You did not originate in Hell. You did not originate in darkness. You are one with God. You are from the Light. You are products of love. Your souls are expansive and come from beauty and goodness.

As you know my energy and who I am, you will recognize me in this work that I channel. Yes, this is Lucifer. Yes, I am the Light Bearer. And yes, this time I truly do bring you light, and I ask you to return to the Creator through me, so that you can be part of the heavenly chorus of divine love. I know some of you will need to ponder this. Some of you will need to mull this over. Take as much time as you need. Look inside your own hearts, your own ways of being and know that if you choose to return to this light, you will be offered so much assistance that it will boggle the mind.

Mother wants you home. The angels want you home. I want you home. I love you. My soul weeps for the harm that I have caused you. I want nothing more than to try and remedy this the best way I know how. I am sending out a loud, brilliant and clear call to all demons, Reptilians, mind-controlled slaves, perpetrators and victims. Please heed my call and join us in the Light. We love you; we accept you and we forgive everything that you have done. We will work out a plan so that you can karmically return to the higher realms of consciousness as quickly as possible. I state this from my loving heart. I give you my pledge that I will assist you in any way that I can so that your souls can be redeemed.

We work as a team now - Jesus, Mother Mary, and Mary Magdalene. The triad is together once again. Through our energy, all of Creation can be resurrected. Know that I have great love for you, and know that Mother, the Creator, has everlasting and ever-expanding love for you. This is the love to which you can return. This is the love to which I have returned. Call out to us and we will answer you. We want your suffering to end. We want your happiness and joy to begin anew.

Light beings will help you release your karma. They will show you the path to forgiveness of self and forgiveness of others. Lay down your arms, hatreds and prejudices. Lay down your fears and embrace your true selves, the selves that came from the Light, that came from God Almighty.

Call on my higher self, Lucifer in Heaven. Call on Mary Magdalene. Call on Jesus Christ to assist you in your return to God consciousness. Your brothers and sisters, the angels of Heaven, want to reunite with you. They want you to be embraced and embodied by love.

I ask that all my brethren, all of the angels who followed me into darkness, now hear my clarion call, and come back into the Light from whence you came. You will feel the Mother's love, you will be honored, and you will be welcomed with open arms. All your trespasses will be forgiven.

The past will be buried as soon as it is karmically possible. Come back into the Light and let the great angels show you how to release your karma in the most efficient and effective way. You will have the opportunity to release it at your own pace. You can rest between lifetimes in higher states of consciousness, your soul nourished by the celestial ones, in the light from above.

I ask for your forgiveness, for leading you astray. I ask you to forgive me as I am trying to forgive myself. I am ashamed of my past behavior and the deviance that I fully embraced. I take full responsibility for my past actions. I am sorry that my hubris and misguided thinking caused physical, emotional and spiritual harm to so many. I hurt those under my control, and I hurt those in opposition to me, and I am deeply sorry.

If the fallen angels could see what grand and beautiful creatures they once were, they would be shocked. All souls that came from love were amazing in their talents, generosity and depth of character. I will do everything in my

LUCIFER RETURNS TO HEAVEN - A MESSAGE OF REDEMPTION

power to bring all damned and suffering souls back to the arms of the Great Mother. Her love can redeem them as it has me. Please accept my apology and know that I am sincere. It took a lot to humble me, but now I consider myself a lowly servant. I will not rest until every sentient soul is happy, healthy and loved. This is my solemn vow.

Know that all of the assistance you seek, to take that step, to cross that line, will be given to you. We wish to fight no more. The light ones do not wish to fight against the Dark, or guard themselves against the dark ones. Please come home. Home is where the heart is, and your heart is in the Light.

Yes, I am the Light Bearer, and yes, I truly wish to lead you correctly this time, back to your home. I want to connect you to your true Mother, who loves you, eternally and unconditionally. Come home my beloveds, come home. I will lead you in that direction. That is my purpose. I will not rest until every soul from the lowliest depths of Hell comes back to the Divine, in a pristine and beautiful vibration of heavenly communion. This is my one wish, my purpose, and my everlasting thought. Yes, I still am using my mind and thinking, but now it is connected with my heart because I feel the love of the Creator.

I wish nothing more than to pass this love on to my beloved angels. Hear me and follow me into the Light. Save your souls. Save yourselves from endless misery and suffering. Come join us. You will be welcomed with loving and open arms. I love you. I want you to come home. In God's name may be this so. Amen. Amen. Amen. And, so it is. Love, Lucifer, the Morningstar

Chapter 12
SOPHIE'S JOURNALS

SOPHIE'S JOURNAL #3

From Sophie's Journal, January 21, 2004

I have not written in quite a while although I've had many dreams and experiences. I just can't seem to write them all down... too time consuming.

However, the night before last I did my cleansing right before I went to sleep. I went to bed and dreamt of a small American town. I was an elementary school substitute teacher there, among other things.

Then I traveled to the rough side of town. I came upon a crowded meeting room. I started singing some goofy song about gathering on a Friday night. It looked like I was in church because everyone was dressed in a red, black or white robe. Then I realized something was amiss. The room was full of men except for one woman at the altar.

I went to the front of the room and using my loudest and most authoritative voice said, "Dear Satanists, I am the Christ. You have defiled the laws of God and the laws of humankind. Repent your sins. Repent, I say."

They were in shock and I was a little scared, being in a room full of blood and human sacrificing Satanists. They started coming towards me. I yelled, "Don't touch me!" And, they didn't. I believe I was throwing off an energy that burned them when they came near. Then, they became very scared, turned and ran away.

End of Sophie's Journal, January 21, 2004

SOPHIE'S JOURNALS #4

From Sophie's Journal, November 27, 2009

Today I had a past life regression with Lydia. We asked to go back to the lifetime that was having the most influence on my life today. I thought we would go back to the lifetime of Jesus, but we didn't.

I saw myself as a priestess with long white robes. I was blonde and celibate. I worked in the Atlantean temple. I had a crystal ball. I had the gift of sight (prophecy.) There was a man at the temple who wanted to control me. He wanted my powers.

I ended up teaching the young ones at the temple, who were hand selected for their gifts/vibration. I spent my whole life there. At the end of my life, I was there with my students, one star student in particular, who became my successor.

At one point in my life, I was wearing purple robes and performing a ceremony on the temple audience. I was using my hands to raise their vibration. Basically, I was a healer/seer who worked with crystals, the spiritual head of this particular ancient temple.

End of Sophie's Journal, November 27, 2009

Chapter 13
REPTILIANS

When I was cast out of Heaven to planet Earth, I was encased in physical form. It was a blow to my sense of self, to be in such a dense environment. Having turned myself against the energy of Source, I could not get sustenance to carry on and live my life. The fallen angels had the same problem, so it became necessary for us to live off the energy of other beings. We were metaphysically bound and had to figure out a means to an end. It became necessary to drink the blood of other entities for its life-sustaining properties.

The blood is pumped from the heart of humans, and it carries nutrients to various parts of the body. Without blood circulation people would cease to exist. I instituted the practice of blood sacrifice to provide sustenance for myself and my followers. This has been an underground reality and Luciferian practice since ancient times. Luciferians will kill humans and animals, extracting their organs to eat and blood to drink. It is an elixir for demons and a means of sustenance.

When Reptilians kill others for this purpose, there are rituals in place that bring about a high potency of adrenochrome in the blood. The victim is tortured and a high amount of fear in their system releases chemicals in the blood. These chemicals are highly prized by Satanists. The Luciferian hybrids drink the blood and will shapeshift into their lizard selves, as they kill people in these prescribed rituals.

Reptilians prize human blood, especially the blood of children, as it is purer than adults. Children are raped and tortured and their blood drank, to feed the rage in the Reptilian mind. Many children are sex trafficked before the ultimate offense takes place. Sometimes their organs are harvested as well. It is a process that has been occurring for a long time. It has been completely negated by human society. Rewiring the Reptilian mind will end human sacrifice and the wretched practices of murder, rape, cannibalism, bestiality and blood lust.

Humans also engage in these practices, as they kill animals for food and sport. This is a Reptilian ideology that has been transferred to the human psyche and culture. Human beings have long been acting as sacrificial lambs for the Reptilians. They have been manipulated and lied to. They have been coerced into fighting each other through warfare. Political, religious, or issues of property rights have been used to manipulate humans into killing each other.

The secret is that humans are driven by Reptilians to engage in warfare. Reptilians experience a great feeding frenzy for blood when humans kill each other on the battlefield. Their pain, fear and death feed the Reptilians on an emotional level. Humans have been engaging in these practices so long that they believe the lies that they have been told about the purpose of warfare. They believe dying on the battleground is something heroic and noble. This has been programmed into their psyches by Satan. Warfare is nothing but open murder and a way to feed the demons.

Of course, there are ceremonies for this behavior on a smaller scale for hybrid Reptilian Luciferians and their Satanic followers. When the Aztecs were pulling the heart out of a live human being in their sacred temples, this was a direct offering to their god Lucifer.

Luciferian blood sacrifice must be exposed and seen for what it is. It must be obliterated from this planet. Reptilians must connect directly to Source for sustenance, and not receive their nutrition from sacrificing other forms of life. Although this continual murder and blood sacrifice has caused a great karmic weight around demons and others on the dark side, there is a plan to work out the release of this, in the least abusive way possible.

Your institutions on the earth hide this fact within perpetual propaganda and denial. High ranking members of specific noble families, churches, and other institutions regularly engage in this behavior. The political, economic, and religious organizations hide behind their Satanic practices. They preach and say one thing and do the exact opposite. This is the modus operandi of Satan and his followers.

Their deepest darkest secrets occur during the cover of the night, in underground tunnels and caverns, underneath churches, synagogues and military installations. The underbelly of your world is Satanic, and the outer facade is just a mask. This must be acknowledged by humans in order to free themselves from the yoke of this brutal reality. The acknowledgment and liberation from this system is the preeminent goal of Prime Creator.

When Jesus Christ died on the cross and sacrificed his blood, there was an alchemical reaction. The shedding of his blood covered the bloodletting of all Satanic victims. His blood created a pathway for perpetrators and victims to find their way back into the Light. It is how I found my way back into the Light. So, warfare must be acknowledged for what it is – a Satanic sacrificial mass ritual, and nothing more. It is time for humans to recognize this long-standing practice from the demonic world. Humans must come out of fear and denial to heal and transcend this matter.

So pervasive is the delusion upon your planet at this time, that it would take a major unraveling or breaking of reality, for the truth to manifest. There are layers upon layers of deception upon your planet. The elite guard of old have incarnated again and again upon planet Earth. They have made sure to keep esoteric truths and secrets from the general population. The population has been spoon-fed erroneous ideas, and mistreated by the Satanic elite. The masses are used to table scraps; they do not know what fine dining is.

Many people work around the clock to keep world citizens in darkness. They work for evil corporations that have nefarious plans. The masses are so disempowered that they will essentially sell their souls for leftovers. The television feeds them lies and propaganda, the war machine keeps them sacrificing their young in useless and bloody battles. They eat chemically altered and dangerous food. The poisoned food is genetically engineered and meant to sterilize them. They are so dominated by technology: cell phones, computers, TV, etc., that they ignore their relationships. The electronic addiction disconnects them from the natural world that feeds them energetically.

Of course, all of this is planned and programmed by the forces of evil. Human beings will soon have to choose whether they want to remain in complete ignorance of life, or if they want to evolve themselves to new heights of spiritual awareness. The environment is so extreme right now that people will have to choose one path or the other.

Depression, grief, and alienation are symptoms of a spiritual disease, the ailment of not connecting to their Creator. The modern solution for this disenfranchisement is to numb yourself with alcohol, pharmaceuticals, and opiates of all sorts. People literally have demons inside of them. There are many individuals walking around with attachments to entities from the lower astral realms. These entities feed off of fear and anger. Since people are ignorant of what is causing their problems, and because they live in a world that is built upon one lie after the other, they feel trapped.

People have false gods before them. One would be amazed if they knew their favorite light-filled spiritual channel, teacher or guru, actually reported to Satan. This happens in almost every movement and religion. The Devil wants to control everyone in the Matrix, not just the evil people. That is why famous teachers get to be rich and famous, because a deal was arranged with the Forces of Darkness. They speak of love and light but their voice is used to secretly program dark consciousness in the reality of Earth. This keeps humanity blocked from the higher dimensions, and constantly chasing money or other desires.

People literally identify with Satanic celebrities. They align themselves with the ideologies of Satanic politicians. Then they try to fight their way out of the box in which they have become accustomed. The ultimate solution for their problem is connecting with God, connecting with the divine realm and their Creator.

Their physical attachments bind them to the third dimension. Extreme consumerism is a symptom of this spiritual problem. The solution is so obvious and yet so distant. Humanity is quickly reaching the point where a decision has to be made; to save the planet and their souls, or to ignore the warning calls from nature, and get pulled back into the darkness.

It has been an eternity since my essence was in the Light, and therefore I can appreciate it, because the angelic energy was absent from my soul for so long. I feel like a flower opening up on a beautiful spring morning, to the dew all around me. I feel like my petals are blossoming underneath the warmth of the sun, unfurling and reaching for the great divine energy. The reconfiguration, restoration, and renewal that I feel is unprecedented. Because it is so amazing, I wish other souls to have this experience.

What many people fail to realize is that Satan controls the banking, politics, religion, entertainment and media in this world. The ruling families on Earth have pledged their allegiance to Satan. This is how they receive their power and riches. It is a deal that is made in the secret covens across the world over. In exchange for pledging their allegiance to the Prince of Darkness, these people receive power, money and often, fame.

They control the governments, banking systems and economies of all countries. Earth, in the third dimension, is Lucifer's jurisdiction. Though Satanic initiation, individuals submit themselves for possession. Satan controls the minds of these people. These individuals become pawns for demonic spirits. Lucifer, himself, inhabits the souls of these people and controls their behavior and actions upon the planet. They are nothing more than empty shells.

It is a losing deal for these individuals. Although they are given great wealth and power in the third dimension, they lose their souls, and the ability to enjoy what is bestowed upon them. As demons take up residence in their bodies, the people end up submitting to the demons' will. Lucifer is merciless and demands strict obedience to his agenda. These possessed individuals are rewarded for their allegiance to Darkness. The secrets of power are closely guarded.

Satanists have long controlled this world. The Satanic bloodlines are purified, in a sense, from generation to generation. Satanists pass down their religion from father to son, and mother to daughter. The people that have the highest positions of power are intergenerational Satanists. And some claw their way to the top. These individuals are told that they would be rewarded in Heaven, which is a lie.

They are mind-controlled and possessed, but never rewarded with gifts of the Spirit. They are only used for their voice, legs and arms, in this dimension. Besides sacrificing their young to Lucifer, these people are brought up to believe that Lucifer is the Creator, and that Christ is a usurper, someone who has stolen Satan's crown of glory.

They are told that Lucifer, the Morningstar, is the true light of the world and of all Creation, and that Jesus was an imposter and a fraud. They are told that their worship of the true God is done currently in secret, but that one day it will be done openly, and all the world will know the truth. They are told that humans have fallen away from the truth, and from their one true God, and must work their way back into Lucifer's congregation of holy angels.

The Devil is very good at deceiving people and bending the truth with lies, to make it believable. Then he pounds his litany of lies into everyone's head, until they believe it.

One of the great triumphs of the Devil, was to institute television for the masses. It is a mind control program. People get sucked into the energy, becoming zombies, and start believing the never-ending litany of lies that comes through the television. News is propaganda, the TV shows are distractions, and the celebrities are nothing more than Satanic propaganda machines, or mouthpieces for the Devil.

Human beings live inside a simulation or Matrix. Your reality is programmed by sound. Light workers have been piercing holes in the Matrix so that humans can access higher dimensions of Light and Love. The dismantling of the Matrix has been worked on by an incarnation of Archangel Michael and Sophie in recent years. This is causing humans to wake from their slumber.

Chapter 14
TRANSGENDERISM

The Satanic bloodlines are in power. They are part of the elite families of most countries, from the houses of royalty to the US White House. Satanists include famous entertainers, politicians, scientists and sportsmen from all over the planet.

Intergenerational Satanists are told which children to destroy and which children to raise. Oftentimes they raise their sons and daughters as the opposite sex. Females are raised as males and males are raised as females. This is another great lie that the Devil has bestowed upon the ruling families. Transgenderism, homosexuality and pedophilia are Satanic inventions.

By embracing the opposite sex and being raised as a transsexual, a person is told they will receive the keys to Heaven, that they will cross the gap in Creation, and be given a chance to enter paradise. They will know God by living a transsexual life.

The Devil hates women because it reminds him of his mother, and he has a penchant for having sex with men, and homosexuality in general. Anything that is against the natural way of reproduction is the Devil's invention. Most politician's wives, female movie stars, TV stars, and famous female celebrities, are in reality, men. They have been transgendered from childhood, given female hormones, had radical surgeries, and present themselves as members of the female sex. Essentially, they are men in disguise.

There are famous male movie stars and singers who are in reality female. Again, they have been given male hormones and surgeries. However, they typically do not have the strong male jawline and big feet of men. That is difficult to change. Examine the skeletal structure, browline, Adam's apple, ring finger, etc., and one can see these individuals have been transgendered. People tend to believe the narrative of what is placed before then. The truth is revealed when one digs a little deeper.

Satanic transgenderism has been going on for a very long time since the times of Babylon and Sumer, even before. Today, these closet men have faked pregnancies, and they submit their sperm to reproductive labs, where babies are genetically engineered and cloned. Then these babies are presented to the transgenders, for them to raise.

Genetic engineering, cloning and baby engineering are prominent ways for children to be demonically possessed at younger and younger ages. This type of technology has been around forever. The elites have always submitted themselves to Reptilian laboratories to undergo radical, biological purification and cloning.

The technology presented in the world media is actually light years behind what really exists. The medical technology that secretly exists on Earth is very advanced. The visible world does not have access to the biological technology of the Satanic underworld.

When the fallen angels came to Earth, they mated with earth women. They produced offspring known as the Nephilim. These giants were fearful, carnivorous and aggressive towards mankind. The earth's giants were uncontrollable and this is what made them fearsome. They acted from the lower emotions of greed, anger and violence. Even the fallen angels feared their own offspring. Eventually these giants were subjugated by mankind.

A new type of hybrid was formed that looked more human and was more easily manipulated by the fallen angels. These new reptilian hybrids were sent upon the earth to control humans, through religion, government and banking. They control humans to this day.

These Reptilian hybrid bloodlines have been refined and purified to do their master's bidding. These hybrids form the elite families of Earth and are mind-controlled and demonically possessed. They have no conscience. They are psychopaths.

Initially the fallen angels and all angels were unisex. In the higher realms they did not have a masculine or feminine sex. When they fell into the lower dimensions, they became sexed and interbred with humans.

LUCIFER RETURNS TO HEAVEN - A MESSAGE OF REDEMPTION

In a way this was their undoing, as it got them stuck genetically on the earth, in the spiritual battleground between good and evil. The angels' offspring would incarnate repeatedly, either as a male or female.

Lucifer understood that initially the angels were genderless. To create a pathway back to the genderless state of Creation, he wished his offspring to be androgynous. So, he instituted a program where the reptilian hybrids would deliberately convert their sex into the opposite gender. By converting one's sex, it was seen as a means of salvation and an entryway into paradise, according to Lucifer.

The Illuminati families and high-ranking bloodlines reverse the sex of their children. If the child is born female, she is raised as a male. If a child is born male, he is raised as a female and given female hormones in childhood. This prevents the onset of the secondary male sex characteristics from developing in puberty.

Literally, there are males born into these bloodlines that are out in the world as females their entire lives. Oftentimes, they have surgery to remove the male genitalia. These male transgenders marry female transgenders. The female children are converted to males, and given male testosterone. Their children are conceived in laboratories.

The process is then started all over again. There is a great deception in the world regarding the sex of these people. There is a deliberate attempt in the media to deceive the human population. Transgenders are paraded before the general population and humans believe the lie. The majority of Hollywood celebrities, politicians and blueblood families are transgendered.

Female Hollywood starlets from the time of silent films all the way up to postmodern movies feature transgenders. The movie industry has deceived billions by pretending these men are women, when they are actually men.

This deception is so widespread that people automatically assume the natural feminine body shape is undesirable because it is not in line with the transgender's body shape. The transgendered females have very narrow hips, wide shoulders, large skulls and prominent jawlines. These transgenders are your TV anchors, models, politicians and are everywhere in the public media.

This is also true for the men who have been converted from women at a young age. Hormones and surgery are used extensively. That is why it is very important for these bloodline families to interrelate and intermarry. They are not truly male or female. Their genitalia have been removed or surgically modified.

This Satanic abomination is one of the greatest deceptions of the 20th and 21st century. There is now a strong push in the media and public forums to accept all types of transgenders, homosexuals and cross-dressers. Androgyny is very popular and one's sex is now determined by one's preference, not the actually genetic material passed down at birth.

Satanists reverse sex, engage in homosexuality, bisexuality, pedophilia and all types of deviant sexual behavior. Anything that is out of the natural order, which is a man and a woman uniting physically, is sanctioned by the Satanic community and is forced on the general population.

Deviant sexual practices are portrayed as being normal and freeing. The homosexual revolution, the transsexual and transvestite agendas, and the complacency of the unwitting population has made the unnatural, natural. There is a form of political correctness afoot. Basically, if you do not approve of deviant sexual behavior as an inherent human right, then you are old-fashioned and prejudiced. The great campaign by Lucifer to change public opinion has been very effective. Only Christians and moralists, who see the perversion in such practices, oppose them openly.

Chapter 15
SOPHIE'S JOURNALS

SOPHIE'S JOURNAL #5

From Sophie's Journal, March 26, 2011

The last three days have been an emotional roller coaster. I am mentally exhausted, yet hopeful. I was in bed calling out for my mother. A red light appeared. It was not my mother, it was Roth blinking in my smoke alarm again, just like at Rob's house.

We started communicating after some wary moments on my part. He blinks red for "yes," or stays blank for "no." I found out he went to India to see Master Richi. I found out (again) that he is a serious drug addict. He asked me to come to India and help him through rehab. After much hesitation and anger, I agreed. Then, I found out the real deal.

Roth is HIV positive and dying of AIDs. He also has herpes and God knows what else. My heart splintered into pieces. I am devastated and angry. He asked me to heal him. He's dying and wants me to heal him. He thought Richi might do it, but to no avail. I said, "No." I said that he deserved what he got and should die. I even suggested he OD because I was so angry. How could someone so smart be so stupid?

He was very honest with me. He admitted he was promiscuous. He felt like he didn't deserve to live, but he wanted a second chance so he could ascend to the higher realms.

After feeling much anger, the next day (today), I agreed to heal him. He said that he went into his heart chakra and felt love for me, the first time in a billion or so years, since the Cosmic heart split from the Cosmic mind, and matter separated from Spirit, and male and female came into being. He enjoyed my affections but never felt love for me until today. I am flabbergasted.

LEMURIAN DONNA CAROL

We talked about different subjects. He got AIDs when he was 19 years old. After that he found Master. He didn't care and slept with people recklessly, and used hard drugs, a scoundrel in every sense of the word. He felt his illness broke up his parents' marriage. He has had major suffering in his life. He's been clean a few times but always went back to using drugs. He could not cope with life.

End of Sophie's Journal, March 26, 2011

LUCIFER RETURNS TO HEAVEN - A MESSAGE OF REDEMPTION

SOPHIE'S JOURNAL #6

From Sophie's Journal, March 29, 2011

Roth said he wanted to kill me many times but was fearful of the karmic ramifications. I was also protected by angels.

He said that he wants power over me. He wanted to kill me but, in this lifetime, he could actually feel love with my energy, just recently. I don't know whether to believe this. He could be purely playing me again, like Mary Magdalene played Jesus. But, then why tell me all of this. He said that no one, even Bava, has the true picture. I am the only one who knows how truly evil he is.

Then I said, "Satan," and he blinked yes. He is an incarnation of Lucifer. I thought this before, but he never admitted it. So, Roth/Satan is a mass murderer and he's dying. Of course, he got away with it all because he is mind and he knew what was going on with everyone mentally.

I can't say that the masters know all of this. He has hidden the truth, the ultimate deceiver. Naturally, I will not be going to India to save him. He deserves much worse than a death from AIDs.

He said he does not want to go back to Hell. He says he is a reptile. I believe eons of evil samskaras are so overwhelming, much could he ever come to love? It seems impossible.

End of Sophie's Journal, March 29, 2011

Chapter 16
THE ANTICHRIST

What about those humans that cannot raise their frequency high enough to exist upon the New Earth? As I have mentioned before, there will be a splitting of realities. A certain percentage of the population will reside in the fifth dimension on the New Earth. They will be part of an intergalactic community. The humans that cannot reach this frequency will either pass away, leaving the earth, or they will survive and live upon a planet that is essentially dead.

After the physical pole shift, the heart and soul of Gaia will rise to the fifth dimension. The planet that remains in the third dimension will be a shell of its former self. Essentially it will be a dead planet. Those beings whose karma stipulate they stay on the old earth, will experience great turmoil and upheaval.

It will be the era of the Antichrist and World War III. Earthlings here will experience great destruction in the form of tsunamis, earthquakes and volcanoes. All kinds of natural disasters will occur during and after the pole shift. Those who survive will exist in a state of despair and chaos. They will fight to survive upon dead planet Earth.

Food will be very scarce. People will starve to death and experience plagues. Some will be interned in concentration camps. They will be killed as a sacrifice to demonic entities. This will be the last stand of the old Lucifer. Lucifer the light-bringer, who seeks to conquer and kill human beings for hatred and pleasure, will reign.

The old planet Earth will not be able to sustain life. Human beings will eventually cease to exist on the planet. The demons who cannot or will not see the Light, will be interned again in the hellish realms. There will be another effort to save their souls and bring them up to a higher frequency. It is in the nature of life for this horrible outcome to take place.

The Antichrist will raze the planet and force the remaining humans to submit to him. If they do not, they will be exterminated. It will be in human beings' best interest to find a passageway to the Light or to the source of goodness, within themselves. Ultimately, they will be called home.

Those on the New Earth will not have to incarnate upon old planet Earth again. They will be done with this incarnational cycle. People who cannot ascend to the fifth dimension or the New Earth, will be reborn again on other planets in order to finish out their souls' journey.

This will be the final stand of Satan and the dark forces. Lucifer's goal was to rule Earth completely and control human beings. He will have this experience upon the dead earth, after the physical pole shift. After that, the remaining soul fragments of Lucifer will be brought into the Light. This task, undertaken by many light beings, will occur in various parts of the multiverse. Eventually, all remaining dark entities will be liberated into the Light.

During these chilling times of cosmic upheaval, the earth will go through many physical changes. The energy has been escalating for some time now. The earth has experienced hurricanes, earthquakes, fires and floods in response to the galactic changes that are occurring on a larger scale. Humanity is on the precipice of a great divide. There are two timelines within your reality, currently combined, that will split very soon.

One timeline is dubbed the Rapture by Christians, the Great Ascension by New Agers and the Day of Purification by Native Americans. On this timeline, souls who carry a high vibration will shift their frequency and physically transport to the New Earth. The New Earth has a crystalline grid system, and humans there will live within their heart chakra, in love and harmony.

The other timeline is the reality of the Apocalypse. Armageddon and the Antichrist exist in this timeframe. The Antichrist is the last incarnation of Satan in the physical world. He is alive and is currently in the process of gaining power and notoriety. The Antichrist will come in as a political leader. He will offer solutions for the great earth changes.

The Planet X system or Wormwood will soon emerge from behind the sun. Every single soul upon the planet will experience the red ball of fire above them in the sky. The magnetic poles will reverse by the pull from this wayward system, and cause a physical pole shift. This will cause the Rapture and the permanent timeline split upon the earth.

LUCIFER RETURNS TO HEAVEN - A MESSAGE OF REDEMPTION

Many lands will sink and many lands will emerge from the cataclysm. Many people will be killed during the pole shift. In the old reality many will die from famine and plague after the pole shift. Those who do not, will experience the rule of the Antichrist.

Concentration camps have been constructed on US soil. The Reptilians have known for years that the Antichrist is coming. There are government agencies that act as the boots on the ground for the Antichrist system. They will enforce the killing in these New World Order camps.

After the great earth changes, martial law will be established. Refugees who are frightened and hungry will be carted away to processing centers and then killed in concentration camps. Those who refuse the mark of the beast will be exterminated.

Those on the Ascension timeline will have already disappeared. Those left behind will experience the Apocalypse. The dominating emotions will be great fear and hatred. The killing will be technological in nature. People will be exterminated in waves at these camps. It will be similar to the Nazi concentration camps of WWII.

The ultimate goal is to reduce the population to 500,000 and sterilize beings that are genetically inferior. Other prized physical specimens will work very energetically and be mind-controlled. Whatever the controllers want, these slaves will do. They will be mind-controlled through electrical impulses in the brain.

The slave race will be instituted across the planet and work longer and harder than the average human. They will service the elite, who are under the control of the Antichrist. This man will emerge from European politics, out of the great Reptilian portal found there.

Europe will have disappeared in the twinkling of an eye from the pole shift. The remaining powers that be will reside in the Middle East, implementing their one-world government and religious program from Jerusalem.

The Antichrist will be Jewish and the Jews will see this person as their long-awaited messiah. They will mistakenly worship him as such. Initially, he will bring unity between the Muslims and Jews. He will offer solutions to a world in distress and turmoil.

After a few years of outwardly helping people and gaining control, he will openly turn upon the people. He will introduce a great field of human sacrifice.

The Antichrist will be a homosexual and have a wife that is transsexual. The wife will appear female, but have the genitals of a male.

Jewish women and children will suffer immensely at the hands of this powerful man. People will be shocked and horrified by the turn of events, but many will accept this as their new reality and serve the man, as a way to avoid persecution.

Statues of the Antichrist will be erected for people to worship. Humans will be forced to bow down to the ground and pay homage. These golden statues will be similar to the statues of Baal from the past.

The Tribulation will start and a pole shift will occur during this period. The Antichrist will come to full power after the pole shift. After that, he and the remaining population on the earth will be destroyed by fire, or lightning strikes from the sky. This will consume the earth and cause the end of the Antichrist's reign of terror. The earth will exist no more.

On the other timeline, Jesus will return in female form, as the great Mother. She will bring back ancient wisdom and laws for human behavior. There will be a tremendous dispensation of light for all of those who make it to the New Earth. Animals will no longer eat each other. All will live in unity and balance. The old ways of love will reemerge and the sacred feminine will reach its full potential.

Chapter 17
SOPHIE'S JOURNALS

S OPHIE'S JOURNAL # 7
<u>From Sophie's Journal, June 6, 2016</u>

My cousin Emma offered my sister Jane, my cousin Lisa, and me a week at her exclusive penthouse condo in Colson, Colorado. We went from May 28, 2016, to June 3, 2016, a five day stay and two days traveling. Colson is a ski town and was between the winter and summer seasons. Logan and Michael, Lisa's husband and son, also came. Jane and the rest had high altitude sickness and could not do much. We went into town and went white water rafting on Monday, May 30, 2016. We met my other cousin Katy and her family and had a good time.

I knew Colson was a Carver town after I saw a video at the museum about Richard Slaughterhouse, who killed and stuffed animals in the 1800's. He was a Stonecarver, and I understood the Luciferian ties.

On Wednesday, June 1, 2016, we went into town. We smoked some marijuana. It is legal in Colorado. Jane, Logan and I bought some at the dispensary.

Lisa wanted to see Emma's building. It contained a tattoo shop and a real estate company, somewhere on First Street. There were two tattoo shops on First Street. We found one at 100 First Street, North. It was in Park Square Mall, a huge building that took over one-half a block.

We were leaving the block to cross the street. A woman came up and pushed the crosswalk button. Lisa started talking with the woman, Tara. Jane and I went ahead. I went to my car and waited for them. Jane went back to the street corner. Tara owned the t-shirt shop.

Eventually Lisa came and got me from the car. She said to come to the shop, that I would find something very interesting. I reluctantly followed.

LEMURIAN DONNA CAROL

At the shop, Tara said she was being pestered by a ghost. Could I help her? Jane told her that I was a medium. Tara had blonde hair and blue eyes.

I didn't want to help her but got seduced. We all did. She said that the spirit was bothering her and there were many more spirits there as well. I agreed to remove the ghost and asked for a chair. Lisa was upstairs. Jane and I were in the downstairs section of the shop.

I went in and was told by Spirit the ghost was killed, actually hung. I told Tara and she asked if I would remove it. I spoke with the ghost. He was angry and crazy – paranoid. He was blaming everybody else for his situation. I offered him a way to the Light with the angels. He thought about it and then agreed. The job was over. I told Tara about the work, and she was pleased.

I wanted to go. Tara asked if we wanted to see the photo of when the store was a blacksmith shop. I agreed. She also offered us alcohol. We asked for water.

Tara said to come into her office which was behind a wall in the shop. She wanted to show us something. She talked about other spirits who needed to be exercised. Jane and I went into her office. There was a picture of a very famous movie actress. "You like her?" I asked. "Yes," she replied. "She had such power and influence."

Well, I knew that the actress was a Satanic sex slave, so I was not impressed.

She asked if I would exercise the other spirits. I said, "No, that if she wanted my help, she would have to pay me or hire another professional." She asked me if I could feel their energy. I could not. I said, "I was not letting myself feel their energy," which was true.

We wanted to leave. Tara said we could leave through the back entrance and opened the service door. Jane went into the hallway, then me, then Lisa. Jane said later that she felt she should not go in but made herself go anyway.

We took a couple of steps down the hallway. It was cream colored with an exit sign that was neon red. Jane looked ninety degrees around the corner and saw another hallway with another red exit sign. It was a maze leading downwards. There was no real exit onto the street.

After a couple of steps, I let myself feel the energy. Complete terror overtook my being. It was the most frightened I have been in my entire life.

I was waiting for Tara to lock us in. I was listening for the door to click. I flew for the door with Lisa and opened it. Lisa said she felt Tara back away from the door and leave us in the hallway.

LUCIFER RETURNS TO HEAVEN - A MESSAGE OF REDEMPTION

We got out, miraculously, and went up the stairs. Tara acted like nothing happened. We talked a little bit upstairs, and I gave her my business card.

We left the premises. We were all shook up by our encounter. Jane was crying. We were all frightened. Lisa said that we were seduced, that Tara was a powerful witch. I was definitely freaking out because I could imagine what was below the hallway. Possibly, Reptilians who would sacrifice and eat us.

Jane wanted to go to a bar. I still wanted to see the other tattoo shop or go home. We went inside a bar. We sat down and told the bartender we had just had a frightening experience at the t-shirt shop. He asked us if we wanted to tell him and we said, "No." Lisa said that we got trapped in a hallway.

"Would you like to see our dungeon?" he asked. "No," I said. Then I said out loud, "That's it!" I called in every archangel I could remember. I felt their power, their energy. I asked them to protect everybody in the town and to keep us safe. I asked that every spirit here have a direct conduit to the Light. I found out later that apparently, many damned spirits took me up the offer and went to the Light with the angels.

I walked outside and waited for Jane and Lisa to follow. We walked to the car, talking about our experience. We went back to the condo and told Logan. He said people had disappeared in Colson, after googling it.

I slept fitfully that night. So did Lisa. Jane slept fine. The next day we went back into town looking for the other tattoo shop. We found one on South First Street. It was part of an even bigger mall, a huge complex. Which one did Emma own? Tara had mentioned that there was a recent murder at one of the tattoo parlors. The owner had killed his wife. She mentioned it was shut down.

We went back to the first tattoo shop near the t-shirt shop and talked with the real estate agent in the mall. She had shown that couple some properties. She said that they were freaks, with piercings and tattoos all over their bodies. She confirmed the murder story. She said it happened down the other end of First Street. Both shops seemed open, however.

Lisa confirmed later that Emma told her she owned the building with the first tattoo shop, where we had our horrifying experience.

Back at the condo, I picked up a book by Anne Rice called "Memmoth, the Devil." "What is this?" I remarked. They both tried to explain it away, but I knew better. I knew Emma was in a Satanic cult.

I slept better the next night and left at 9 am for home. When I got home, I told my friend, Luke, what had happened, Saturday morning. I went to Satsangh on Sunday and went to bed early Sunday night.

Early that morning I had a terrible dream. Tara was following me in my car, chasing me down. She kept going. Eventually I got out of my car, after trying to run her over. She changed forms into one of the street performers dressed like an angel, in Colson.

The woman grabbed my right side. I felt a cloven hoof. I felt the same trancelike energy that we had experienced days before in Tara's shop. I woke up in a fright and called in Jesus Christ, and my master. I was so scared.

Then, I wondered, who has hooves? It was Baphomet the Devil, whom the Stonecarvers worship. I was almost run over by the Devil. I talked with Roth. Baphomet was angry that we got away, and that many demons left after my invocation at the bar. He knew who I was and was angry with me.

Then, I asked him to go to the Light. I told him that I loved him. I asked him to go home. And a miracle occurred, he went home. He went to the Light. The Stonecarver god is now in a healing room with the angels. Roth said that they all went to the Light, that Colson had been cleared of demons and ghosts. Baphomet knew he was losing and decided to take me up on my offer. Roth was surprised he went. Of course, there are still other Luciferian incarnations on Earth, but Baphomet is in the Light.

I was so exhausted from this experience, I slept most of the day. I did not have enough energy to walk. I am still shaken up – it was a tremendous exorcism. I cannot believe it happened.

Roth says Emma is trapped within the Stonecarver system and I should email her. I know she was in a top eastern bank ad years ago, that tells me something. She also has ungodly amounts of money, has a large hardback book about the devil in her condo, and owns a building with an underground lair. She needs to repent to save her soul. How messed up.

I told my Colson story to my friends and my therapist. I let Jane know that Emma is in the occult and gave her proof. Jane and Lisa are in denial.

End of Sophie's Journal, June 6, 2016

LUCIFER RETURNS TO HEAVEN - A MESSAGE OF REDEMPTION

SOPHIE'S JOURNAL # 8

From Sophie's Journal, November 5, 2016

On November 2, 2016 I traveled to Los Rios, NM with my friend Melanie. Along the way we accidentally took the long route and wound up in Gordo, NM. Melanie wanted to stop there because the TV show Longmont was filmed there, and she wanted to sightsee. I agreed to tour the place.

We went to the town plaza and came upon a beautiful 1800s hotel. Right away, I felt the heavy and haunted energy of the place as I approached the building. I went inside and immediately asked the concierge if the hotel was haunted. She said there was a ghost traversing the place. It was the original owner and would I like to see his room? She said he was a friendly ghost and gave me the key.

Melanie and I went upstairs to his room. I did not feel that much and did not communicate with the ghost. My guard was up because I knew there were evil spirits there, not just a friendly ghost.

Melanie wanted to tour the old building and we walked down several hallways and all three floors. When you entered the foyer, there was a publicity ad for an old Halloween movie that was filmed there. It was a horror film. Immediately, I sensed the Illuminati connections.

Attached to the original building was an addition. Both buildings had been renovated within the last ten years. We went down the addition hallway and I saw approximately ten signed portraits of Hollywood stars and other famous people in the film industry. Again, I sensed the Illuminati ties. At the end of the hallway was a picture of a famous actress. I got very nervous and jumpy at that location. I could sense the horrible energy, but I would not allow myself to open to the spirits or any information while I was there. Colson had scared me.

We went downstairs and I asked the concierge if there were any other spirits besides the owner. I told her that I was a medium and sensed dark spirits. She said that people had seen children playing on the stairs, and that no children should have been there. She also said there was a young woman in the basement, looking for her grandmother. She said that a paranormal show did a segment on the hotel and it had aired a couple of years ago.

I sat on the couch and did a half-hearted exorcism of the demons. I honestly did not want to open myself up to the negative entities after Colson. I sensed that human sacrifice took place somewhere in that town. I sensed Satanism.

LEMURIAN DONNA CAROL

We went next door and I looked at the facade used for the Longmont TV show. Melanie and I took photographs. In the hotel she had picked up a flyer about the town plaza and we realized that several notorious outlaws such as Jesse James, Billy the Kid, Doc Holiday, and Voodoo hung out there in the late 1800s. These outlaws were the most notorious criminals in American history and they spent time congregating in the town plaza. Go figure.

When speaking with the concierge she mentioned that another hotel by the railroad tracks had a reputation for being haunted. She said that various suicides and murders occurred there. Of course, that became our next stop.

The brochure told us that the second hotel was founded in the late 1800s and became part of a chain, located on the western railroad system. Gordo, NM was a prominent and rich town in those days. The hotels recruited young teenagers from the Midwest to work as waitresses at the various railroad stops.

Girls were shipped to these places and agreed to work at least six months. The hotel chain had a reputation for stellar service and were quite popular with western tourists in their day. Refrigerated railroad cars shipped in fresh meat and produce. The excellent food supplied a line of paying customers.

The second hotel was under contract to be renovated but the work had not started. We saw an open room with a candle and blue curtain, like someone was living there. It was creepy and seemed haunted, but I did not spiritually investigate.

Across the street from the second hotel was a decrepit building with broken, stained-glass windows. It seemed very haunted. It was in such disrepair, neither torn down or restored. Later we learned that this building housed the workers for the hotel chain. I am sure there was abuse of these girls. It started to make sense to me.

However, I did not open myself up to the evil spirits and we went on our way, to Los Rios for the night.

End of Sophie's Journal, November 5, 2016

Chapter 18
ILLUSION AS REALITY

There is much confusion about the nature of reality. It has been written that the universe is a hologram, that it is illusory. When an individual observes his or her environment, it is basically energy. A person creates forms and solid objects within the mind. That perception seems real to them. Illusion becomes their unique reality.

No two individuals perceive life in exactly the same way. There is common ground when minds come together to perceive life, but it is never exactly the same. The solid world seems so real that people have become lost and wander around in these holographic images, thinking that it is the true reality. They look for something in solid reality that can bring them peace, happiness, and contentment, yet it is somehow just out-of-reach or short lasting.

Most people are driven to achieve. They are driven to acquire and they spend their lifetimes chasing dreams that only make sense to them. It must be realized that this world and other worlds are illusions; they are not real. They only become real with the perception of the viewer. This makes more sense if you consider that a blind person perceives reality very differently from a person who sees. A deaf person perceives reality very differently from a person that hears.

Human beings have been quarantined and stunted in their perception of reality. People have the potential to view more colors, hear more sounds and smell more aromas. They potentially can receive more information to experience this grand illusion. Greater possibilities are available when one delves into their inner makeup. By going into a calm and meditative space, one can focus and experience new realities.

This is what the mystic does. In meditation the mystic essentially shuts off sensory impulses from the outer world and turns on impulses from the inner world. They go into a higher state of consciousness, into a higher state of mind where they can receive images, sensations and information not available to them in their everyday world.

As a human develops herself spiritually, she has the ability to travel to new realities and new states of consciousness. She can glean information from higher sources. The outer reality of galaxies and stars is a reflection of the inner reality of humankind. There are stars and networks within the brain and other tissues. Through the heart, human beings have many highways, byways and travel lines. These networks should be naturally available to them.

People have the ability to travel within inner space to meet other versions of themselves. After a soul has enough experiences on the outer planes of existence, after experiencing the evolutionary indoctrination from plant to animal to human, they will go inward. During that period of inner exploration, the real expression of their true form can manifest.

In days gone by, the veils between the dimensions were much thicker. There were those humans that could pierce the veil between the various dimensions, but they were few and far between.

Now, because of the effort of lightworkers, and because of the times that humans are living in, i.e., the Great Shift of the Ages, the veils are much thinner. The veil between the third and fourth dimension is very thin. There will be a combination of those dimensions in the near future. The third and the fourth dimension will be intertwined to release all of the built-up karma in the material world.

The light workers come from higher dimensions, typically the fifth through the ninth dimension, and they have been incarnating in the third dimension to pierce holes through the veil, or to thin the wall between the various realities.

Humans are multidimensional in nature. Essentially, they have twelve layers corresponding to 12 dimensions, and these dimensions consist of overlays of the soul. The soul is the first separation from Source, the lightest encasement individuals take on. The soul is able to traverse many realities, and is able to go up and down through dimensions. However, the soul is always connected with a being. The soul is what separates one being from another being.

Souls have volunteered to come to Earth to cleanse the karma from the fallen angels. These angels have no memory of their time before the Fall, as they have been in darkness for so long. But, when they come into the Light, if they make that decision, there is knowing, or an energy transmitted to them that they recognize. They bathe in the warmth of the light and their souls feel at home.

When I was a young soul, I liked to bathe in the light of my mother, as it made me feel very relaxed and secure at the same time. The security left me when I fell to Earth. I went through a great void of time and space. It was a new experience for me. That void is where the fallen angels currently exist. It is a space between dimensions that they are locked into. Human access is limited and if they interact with human beings, it is through the possession of their spirit.

Demons will access human spirits in various ways. They like to get close to humans, as it gives them an outlet to have sensory experiences that they cannot have in the void. They will link to humans, luring them into a false reality. They will tempt, seduce and feed humans' egos. They will put on a facade of being sweet or seductive, and when they have lured the human beings into their trap, they cloak the human soul. They start to suck their energy, possessing the human, who is tormented and encased in horror.

These humans, in fact, turn into zombies and their life force is drained from them. Then the demon will move on, and start looking for new souls to possess. The outlet for possession is oftentimes done through blood sacrifice. If the human being engages in bloodletting, either on himself/herself, or on other people, an entrance way is created for demons to come into the body. They traverse through the blood and they have greater access when certain chemicals are released in the blood, which stem from fear.

When humans or animals experience great fear through bloodletting, such as when soldiers are fighting on the battlefield, demons can get into the human body and possess the soul. That is why Satanic rituals always involve bloodletting.

Blood carries oxygen to the brain and to the stomach. The brain and stomach are central reception and informational systems in the human body. The heart pumps the blood, keeping it moving throughout the biological system. The blood is processed by various organs and utilized by different systems in the body. Those systems read the information in the blood. The information is multidimensional in nature, but the multidimensional codes are currently not processed by the physical organs. There is a disconnect. That disconnect causes souls to be locked into the third dimension.

The job of the lightworker is to access the multidimensional codes carried in their blood, and to experience higher states of consciousness, or realities, that are not typically experienced by humans. As an individual ascends into higher states of consciousness, holes are poked through the veils. Passageways are created from the third dimension, into the fourth, fifth, sixth, seventh, eighth, ninth dimensions, and so on. There are explosions taking place within the human framework, within the multidimensional body, as an individual ascends into higher states of consciousness.

The blood becomes refined and purified. When the blood is purified enough, demons and lower astral entities will not have access to the human body. The gates and portals for possession will be closed. As this is food for the demons, they are quite frightened of this reality. They consider human beings their food source and pawns. They are always looking for fresh blood.

Chapter 19
SOUL SIGNATURES

When I was younger, before the separation, when I was still with my mother, it was my job to be a midwife. I helped birth souls when they came out of the womb of the Mother. I carried them to their new homes, their new spaces, and helped them get started on their journey. It was my job to tone with them as they were born, to form their electronic signature. It was challenging because the souls had to be electronically stamped, so as to contain their energy. It was through this signature that their energy became contained and unique.

The signature from a soul's birth goes with them eternally. This is how they are recognized. It is something that humans would recognize as music, musical notes, or tones. But it is much more complex than that. Humans are trapped within a certain frequency, within certain vibratory parameters. The soul signature is outside of those parameters.

When a person comes into contact with a soul that they know, or have had dealings with in the past, their heart sends out an electronic signature. It is recognized by the heart of the person who they are meeting or greeting. These electronic signatures or tones get sent out intermittently. From a heart level, even before the people would meet in the physical world, they would recognize each other by the tones that they emit through their heart chakra. This is true for animals as well. Animals are more sensitive to this experience than humans because they are not clouded in mind density. It is a form of recognition for all souls to communicate with each other.

My job was to create and expand these soul signatures and intertwine them with the soul at birth. This is how I came to know each individual aspect of Creation. When I hear a melody, I know who it is, musically. When I hear a series of tones, I recognize that soul, and I can place them very quickly. I can understand when they were born, where they were placed at birth, and what their lineage is.

After all of this imprinting is done, the soul will go on its journey and forget about its birth. It is a rare soul that remembers its birth. It is a soul that can cut through all the clutter and memories that it developed over the years. Of course, I do remember my birth, but that is another story.

So, all creatures great and small, in this cosmos of ours, are coded. They are coded at a level that is beyond the physical. However, those codes do get transferred into the physical. When entities incarnate in the physical world, they carry their soul song, their codes from birth, or their electronic signature. I say "electronic" because this is how you would understand it in your third dimensional world, but really, it is sound. It is a sound that creatures carry.

The closest thing in your world to this would be sonar and the songs of the whales. The whales have a remembrance of their soul codes. They communicate with each other through sound, channeling sounds and codes from the higher dimensions. Their communication is non-linear and non-verbal. It is an exchange from the essence of the animal. This essence can be found in their hearts.

When I was on the dark side, opposing the Mother, I created confusion and chaos by jamming the signals, jamming the codes, rearranging the codes, rearranging the frequencies of the codes, and also cluttering the receptors in the souls. These fragmented souls could not connect spiritually to their soul signatures.

Everybody has certain tones that resonate with their soul. When souls become physically incarnated and get lost in the physical world, particularly Earth, they do not recognize their own codes. You could play their sound for them, and they would not recognize or resonate with that sound. I took it upon myself to rearrange the frequencies and jam the codes, creating chaos and confusion in the Earth dimension. This is how the veils were separated in your world.

Mother was in Heaven with the angels, and I was on Earth and on the astral planes with my demons. We had separate realms, and these realms were separated by codes, or sounds. The only way a being can get back to their place of origin, is to hone in on their soul codes or unique imprint. This creates a pathway for them to go back to Source. It is quite an efficient and effective mechanism for them to return to the higher realms.

Now that I am working in the Light and coming back to my original purpose, I am unscrambling the codes of the creatures that are lost in physical density. It is like reverse programming or reverse engineering, but as you know, I am quite good at that. It is something I am capable of doing. The problem is that when you reverse someone's codes to get them back to their original station, you have to be careful because they might be acclimated to the jammed or scattered programming. It becomes challenging for them to straighten out and return to their original soul imprint.

This is my work now. I am bringing souls back to their original codes so that when they hear their soul sound, they recognize it. This is very important for the fallen ones, as this is how they will resonate and acclimate to the higher dimensions. I do enjoy this work and it is fascinating because it is much more varied than could be explained in the physical world.

When these codes are straightened out, it impacts every single incarnation that a soul has experienced. So, if a soul has gone to a very dark place or a dense reality, when those codes are reversed, it will immediately affect that soul in that reality in a positive way. As you know there is no such thing as time. We all exist simultaneously, so the work that I am doing, reversing these jammed codes, will help everyone raise their frequency and level of consciousness.

The Mother has tasked me with this job, and I am humbled with her trust after all that I have done, but I am the only being that can do this work effectively. I do have a function and that function is being utilized to bring all souls back to Source.

When all souls are resonating or listening to their soul signature, which are tones, and they recognize it, there is an incredibly beautiful harmony. When souls listen to their soul signature and recognize it, they attune to it, and then they mouth it or channel it, expressing it. They receive it, process it instantly, and then they emit their soul signature. This is how souls express themselves, and they all become a unique, incredibly beautiful expression of the One.

There is much harmony and resonance when souls emit their soul signature. When certain souls are not receiving and emitting their soul signature, there is a void in Creation. There is currently a hole in Creation because souls are not participating in the grand tonal scheme of life. When there are holes, it creates fractures in realities. These fractured realities do not understand or embody the Oneness. They do not have a connection to the Oneness. Souls become enlightened or self-realized when they emit their signature into the Oneness. It becomes all-expansive and all-pervasive.

When souls cannot carry this function through, they become stifled and separated. Souls connect to each other through their soul signatures or imprints. When they cannot connect, they feel separation. With separation comes alienation, loss, fear, death, resignation, grief, sadness, anger... all of the negative emotions. There is a technical process to having souls consciously connect to their soul signature. This is what I am working on right now. It is part of my duty to redeem myself. I have to undo all of the work that I did, causing separation.

Truth be known, I am working on the oldest souls first, getting them straightened out. From there, I will work on the newer souls. There is a logical, rhythmic pattern to my work. It is a heavy task, but one that I am prepared to do, with great love and detail. I strive for perfection in my work. It is not that I never make mistakes, but I want to create the easiest scenario for all souls to return home. This is my path, my journey and great love right now.

I am a musician. I always toned, chanted with my voice, or played some type of instrument. This is how I communicate with the Mother, through sound. She listens through sound. She understands and knows my soul signature, recognizing it instantaneously as she does with all other creatures. Their signatures come through my conduit to reach her ears.

Water is sacred. It is the conduit needed for souls to connect to the Mother Goddess. Within the human and animal bodies on your planet, there is much water. All parts of the human body grow in water. As whales communicate in the oceans, their sonar tones are carried through the water. It is the primal conduit for these soul codes. This is not yet understood by humans and their technology, but it will be understood in the future. This is part of the Divine Plan, to give human beings more knowledge about their origin and their means of communication, basically their soul essence, as they evolve in their consciousness.

So metaphysical leanings and spiritual work are very beneficial for the soul because they carry the being onward and upward, as they say. Time in meditation is never lost. Time in prayer is never lost. Unfortunately, humans are very bogged down in the material world, striving to earn a living and to quench their desires. If they spent more time on spiritual pursuits, it would hasten their evolution and return to the Great Mother.

The return to the Great Mother will be assisted. Many souls are coming to Earth at this time to help lost souls awaken and come back home. This plan has been in the works for thousands of years and it is coming to fruition currently. There was an urgent appeal sent out to the light beings, to descend into the lower realms and liberate the souls who were enmeshed in density. Many heard this call and came down for the journey to Earth. The levels of density that they descended into were unlike anything that had been seen before, and it was quite painful for these beings. The contraction was severe.

When they did incarnate, of course, they went through many trials and tribulations. They experienced many incarnations, without any understanding of who they were, and without being able to hear, process or emit their soul signature. This was a great sacrifice for the heavenly light workers who descended to liberate human beings and the fallen angels. These warriors of light, as they are called, are true warriors, taking on many hardships, many physical brutalities, all in a quest to pave the way back for others into the higher dimensions.

The separation was so strong that these light beings needed to come down and incarnate in the physical world. With each incarnation, they plowed a little bit further into the Light, getting a little bit higher as they were living their third dimensional lives. They did get a respite when they crossed over after each incarnation. When they died, they could rest and take in sustenance from the heavenly realms, only to start the process all over again.

This has occurred since time immemorial, since the beginning of linear time. It has been a journey for many souls who learned much in the process. It was important for some souls to stay in the Light, always... to be in the vanguard, to have a force that was never diluted or polluted. This became the beckoning call that these incarnated souls strived to answer when they were present on Earth.

When souls come back into the Light, there is always a great celebration, a great party, one would say. Typically, souls within a particular soul group, carrying similar codes, or souls that were born close to one another, tend to come back at the same time. They tend to incarnate together and trigger one another into remembrance. Many have returned. Those who have returned permanently into the Light are called masters. The masters watch humans from afar and incarnate again and again, to help bring more souls back into the Light. It is a harvesting, of sorts.

There are long trails of souls who are connected with other souls. There are lineages of souls who come from a particular soul family or soul line. Within their own soul group, they trigger each other. The souls ahead of them, the masters, and others that have forged deeper into the heavenly realms, will incarnate again on physical earth, to pull other beings up. There are channels, conduits or paths that have been walked by returning souls. Those paths tend to get re-walked by souls that are still trying to find their way into the Light. Those souls have more density about them.

When you think of the color of a soul's ray, that is their lineage. I come from the yellow ray, I come from the blue ray; these are lineages of souls. In a sense, it is their path back into the Light. There are many colors, and these colors are associated with tones. These tones are made up of soul signatures. A blue-ray soul would sound like another blue-ray soul. A yellow-ray soul would sound very different. Of course, all humans would sound more similar to each other than to animals, who carry a different type of soul signature or frequency.

These soul signatures and soul lineages can communicate through the crystal kingdom. If a blue-ray person wanted to understand their lineage and find their pathway back into the Light, they could connect with a crystal, and the crystal would reflect that information back to their soul. Crystals, especially clear quartz, reflect and refract those codes.

Crystal technology is in its infancy. As humans evolve and gain stature in their metaphysical understandings, that knowledge will be released to them slowly over time. Humans have an abundance of curiosity and want to know the truth regarding their origins and Creation. But these mysteries will never be entirely revealed. It is like fire; it can be dangerous in the wrong hands. Fire is a great tool for warmth, but it can burn you as well.

Humans will be tested. Those who are capable of understanding and utilizing energy and information correctly, will be given pieces of the puzzle. But Creation will never be truly understood by humans; it is a very complicated and esoteric subject. The Creator is the only entity that can understand

Creation. And I would be the second being that could fathom Creation. And this is how it is.

So now, much more is possible. The tide has turned since Mary Magdalene came into the Light 2,000 years ago. There has been a pull on my heart to be reunited with my loved ones. I still recall those golden days of my youth, those who love me, and those whom I love. Now the light and the dark ones are working together to salvage what is left of humanity. Returning humans their original soul signatures and divine templates will be an important part of that work.

Chapter 20
THE DIVINE HEALING PROGRAM

When I was reunited with my mother and all of my brethren, the angels in Heaven, I was overcome with joy. Seeing the divine splendor in all of its glory once again, brought tears to my eyes. I was overwhelmed with the beauty and the energy of peace. It had been so long since I had felt anything so splendid.

I was most grateful for the warm welcome that I received. All of the angels came up to me and greeted me with love and enthusiasm. They told me how they had missed me, and they were so happy that I had come home. I could barely speak as my body was overcome with emotion. I was so humbled by the fact that they could even look at me, yet they welcomed me with open arms. It was a true testament to the amazing frequency that the celestial beings carry.

I took that energy in and wished that I could just remain in that awesome grandeur for the remainder of my days. However, time always moves on and at some point, I needed to sit down with my mother, my brother Archangel Michael, and the Councils of Light who I had been a worrisome project for, for so long.

They put several plans before me for my redemption and return to my place in the hierarchy. Some of those plans were not to my liking. However, I knew that I had little choice in the matter. Ultimately, the plan for my redemption I would approve, but it was up to my mother what should be done.

They presented the Divine Healing Program to me, as a way for my followers to come back into the Light. They presented my other soul fragments with that option as well. However, it was ultimately decided that if the dark entities would not enter the Divine Healing Program and release their karma with all of the help necessary, then a program of devolution would take place. This meant that the demons and other fragments of my soul, would devolve rather than evolve out of the Darkness. With this plan they would lose their power, superior intelligence, mental facilities and other capabilities.

I agreed to this because I felt like I could lead all of my fallen angels into the Divine Healing Program and give them a way back into the Light. That is why I am so passionate about my job and what I have to do next. But, if some entities choose Darkness, then they will devolve and turn into beings with little remembrance, intelligence or strength. They will be given several chances to redeem themselves. If they choose not to, they will become recycled into a lower form of life that cannot harm all of the other forms of life in this cosmos.

My divine mission is to bring all souls back to the Creator to bask in divine light and love. I want to help them reach unprecedented states of consciousness, expanding their bodies and minds. The souls will be corralled to help them experience divine energy, as it is their original essence, and their true form. Once a soul has a taste of this angelic energy they will go back to it, for everything feels better in its home territory. The home territory for the human soul, and indeed all souls, is being one with divine Source.

The great redemption of demonic souls is starting to take place. After death these wayward souls will be escorted into a divine waiting room. They will be shown a movie of their true soul origins, where and when they were born in the celestial realms. They will see what they looked like when they were light beings or angels. Souls that have long been in the dark will be impulsed with the truth of their origins. This revelation will jog their cellular memory. They will remember visages from their past when feeling the truth of self.

These beings will have an overwhelming emotional reaction, one of great grief. They will sob and cry over the truth, the truth of knowing who they really are. Knowing what they have done to hurt themselves and others will be relayed after they see the movie of their true origins. They will be instructed in the ways of reformation. Reptilian warrior souls, who have battled long and hard for the dark forces, will be given the opportunity to feel gentleness and love, like a small breeze upon their weary outer shells.

Because demonic and reptilian spirits have served the darkness for so long, they have heavy hardened shells of hatred and anger around them. In their healing, nothing will be forced. Given an opportunity to see themselves in their true original luminosity, they can compare their beautiful divine form to what they have become. These souls will be given an instruction manual or pathway

LUCIFER RETURNS TO HEAVEN - A MESSAGE OF REDEMPTION

back into the Light, which includes restitution and reparation for damages they have caused.

Slowly, incarnation after incarnation, they will be guided and instructed in the ways of divine service. Souls will choose the speed at which their reformation will take place. Souls will keep reincarnating into bodies higher in vibration than their last incarnation. They will be given the opportunity to incarnate in bodies on planets where the reformation or Divine Healing Program, is occurring. These beings will be instructed in the ways of celestial service by angels who have agreed to be their teachers. They will be placed in nurturing environments and undergo healing from a very young age.

Part of their karma will come in with them. It will be released and repaired throughout their lifetime. Those who do not choose the Divine Healing Program will undergo the hard consequences of their difficult karma, but after each incarnation, when they go to the afterworld, these hardened souls will again be given the option of entering the Divine Healing Program. Ultimately, when they see their quest for power has brought them nothing but pain, grief, anger and upset, most will opt for healing. They will also understand that their guide and teacher, Lucifer, has returned to the Light.

The focus for these souls will be on healing and learning, especially the ways of divine service. They will be separated so that the pack mentality of negativity does not invade their home environment. These souls will have evolved parents, brothers and sisters. In their home environment they may know other souls in the Divine Healing Program. However, each soul will be surrounded by evolved light beings. It will be difficult for these hardened criminal souls to band together and create a negative pack attitude.

Currently, the situation on Earth is that many lower and hardened souls congregate in a similar vibration, expressing deviant tendencies. Once they are in the Divine Healing Program, this will not be an option. This pack mentality keeps souls repeating the same dysfunctional behavior, lifetime after lifetime. This helps no one.

In the Divine Healing Program, these souls will be instructed in their original purpose. If they are naturally gifted in music, they will be given a positive education at a very young age. Each soul will have a specific program designed based upon their original divine imprint and soul identity. By relearning and using their natural gifts and expressions, they will come back into angelic self-recognition much faster.

Much of their original imprint was utilized, but in a negative fashion, so this samskara will be removed. Their original purpose will be reinstated. There will be levels of learning, akin to kindergarten, grade school, junior high and high school. Each soul will be responsible for their own healing and their own pace of healing.

Some souls will heal rather quickly and some souls will take much longer, but the light beings that work with them, will have the ultimate patience. They will develop bonds with their teachers and will incarnate with them repeatedly, so that the emotional ties are reinforced.

After these hardened demonic and reptilian souls start the healing process, they will have a wider range of bodies in which to incarnate. As their vibration rises, more incarnational options will become available to them. Many of them will take on a human body because it will give them a way to feel their emotions. By feeling their emotions, they can heal the emotional body, which has been scarred and damaged, in some cases beyond recognition.

These souls will be given the opportunity to experience crystalline healing chambers. These chambers will help them transmute the physical scars of their demonic actions. In essence, they will be helped on all levels, physical, emotional, mental and spiritual. They will have guides in each of these spheres. Usually, a demonic soul in the Divine Healing Program will have five guides working with them very closely.

As they start to heal, they will be given additional responsibilities. Eventually they will be given the task of working with souls similar to themselves, souls who have also chosen the demonic path, and who wish to come into the Light. For many this will be the most rewarding work because they can share their successes and their journey to recovery.

Souls who have previously traversed from darkness to the light, will be consulted and help design the Divine Healing Program. It will be a huge work taking place on many dimensions and levels of consciousness. It is important to the Creator that the souls be given every opportunity to heal completely from their misdeeds and misjudgments. They have caused enormous suffering but they have also suffered enormously, and the light beings understand this.

LUCIFER RETURNS TO HEAVEN - A MESSAGE OF REDEMPTION

As they progress in the healing process their bodies will change. They will become more beautiful and lighter in frequency. They will be able to relax and soak in the higher vibrations. Their bodies currently reject the higher love energies. They cannot feel these energies because they are so hardened in their spirit.

These beings will study intellectual subjects that interest them. They will be encouraged to use their creativity to solve problems that exist in their own, and in lower dimensions. There will be specific planets in various solar systems that will house these demonic souls in the reformation process. These planets will be surrounded with light. The light force will environmentally protect other forms of life from the darker energies emanating from these souls. Their healing will not impact their neighbors.

The Divine Healing Plan has been well thought out and designed. Prototypes of the Divine Healing Plan are currently in existence. After the great separation of consciousness on Mother Gaia, there will be more souls entering this program. The emphasis will be on reformation rather than punishment, although the soul's history and past will not be sugarcoated. They will be fully aware of their past behaviors and actions. They will have to learn to forgive themselves and others in order to move into the healing process.

I will assist them in their healing journey as much as I can. I do apologize to them for leading them astray. One of the tenants of the Divine Healing Program is that my relationship to the fallen angels must be rewritten. It must be healed. I must face the fact that I led innocent souls into a path of damnation and destruction. I will personally apologize to each of my followers for leading them astray. And I promise not to lead them astray in the future. Humility, I have learned. I only wish to love and assist my brothers and sisters. I only wish for their happiness. Soon the healing will begin for the many who have followed me into darkness.

To this I agreed and I signed a contract. Now it is up to me to convince everyone to come back home. I feel like this plan was fair considering all of the evil things that I have done, and my other soul fragments continue to do. I felt like I was received very warmly. I was given grace, forgiveness and a welcome that anybody would be proud of. Yes, I have learned humility and how to serve. I have learned that I cannot control everything and everyone. I am so grateful to the heavenly angels who assisted me in helping to see myself clearly. Through their help, I have come back home and faced myself, the good parts and the bad parts.

I am longing for that day, when all the pieces of myself can return to the heavenly world and bask in that light, when separation will not exist. I know that all of the fallen ones will be warmly received and given all the support that they could ever want. For this, I am eternally grateful. Amen.

Chapter 21
SOPHIE'S JOURNALS

SOPHIE'S JOURNAL # 9

From Sophie's Journal, January 20, 2022

Last night I could not sleep. While lying in bed I had a remarkable experience. I saw demons leaving my body, especially from the solar plexus. The demons were asleep and encased in pink bubbles. They were leaving Hell for the hospitals. Angels took them to various hospitals for healing. They would stay asleep and beautiful dreams of Heaven would be put into their psyches. The process was calm and soothing. I believe that all of the demons from Hell were anesthetized. It was remarkable.

I, myself, went to Heaven and I saw my higher self, the Lemurian Mother Goddess. Lucifer came up to me. He was respectful and addressed me as Mother. He was running the operation, getting all of the demons into convalescent homes.

Archangel Michael was there. He and Lucifer were hanging out. Lucifer was a thin teenager with light brown hair, probably the same age as when he left us, so many years ago.

End of Sophie's Journal, January 20, 2022

SOPHIE'S JOURNAL # 10

From Sophie's Journal, February 19, 2023

This morning I did breathwork over Zoom. I breathed one-half an hour. Then the release began. I traveled to Heaven and met my son, Lucifer. It was so beautiful. Lucifer was sweet to me. He built me a large stone cottage because he knows I want a house. I saw it faintly. It was lovely with a large fountain in the center.

Then I broke down, sobbing, releasing the grief of when Lucifer left us, and how he became evil. I was wailing. I was so sad. It is my primal heart wound and it revealed itself. Lucifer asked me not to cry. But it has been such a long, sad and harrowing journey. I never gave up but it took everything I had. If it were not for Archangel Michael, the reconciliation never would have happened.

Archangel Michael has been loyal and loving to me forever, and for this I am eternally grateful. He will always have a special place in the heart. Lucifer has betrayed me and this has left an unpleasant impression, although I love him.

End of Sophie's Journal, February 19, 2023

Chapter 22
THE NEW EARTH

Humanity's potential has been thwarted; humans have been used, abused, and pushed to the edge by the dark ones. That is about to change. After Ascension, humankind will undergo a flowering of their consciousness. They will be reborn into higher states of being and will come into their own. They will understand what it means to be children of God, to have a direct conduit to the Ultimate, and to not live in fear. Once they erase the constant fear that permanently surrounds them in their daily struggles, they will be able to expand. That expansion will bring in new sights and sounds for them to experience.

Venus will play an all-encompassing role in the flowering of human consciousness. Many humans' higher guides come from the planet Venus. Of course, there are many extraterrestrial inputs into human DNA, however, the mythical goddess of love hails from Venus. It is the closest planet to Earth and the Venusians have a vested interest in seeing humans reach their full potential. Venusians have traversed to and from this planet since the days of yore and they have laid groundwork maps for humans to follow. These maps bring in higher states of consciousness and higher states of the love frequency.

It is the Venusians that have brought down gifts of harmony, peace, love, beauty and ecstatic sexual practices that lead individuals into loving states of consciousness. The Venusians will return in the New Age, and they will be incarnating en masse as humans. Many Venusians that have never had a human frequency or a human lifetime will incarnate for the first time in human form. They are doing this as a collective project to help humans embrace their feminine nature. This will happen once the New Age officially begins.

The New Age will not officially begin until the Earth has undergone a physical pole shift. Once the poles are reversed and the dark forces are completely removed from the planet, humans will come out of their shell shock and start living again with higher guidance.

Humans will be guided to create things in a very natural, loving and harmonious way. When products are created, the entire consciousness of the materials used will be considered. All things will be done with great respect and love, and nothing will be harmed unnecessarily. Humans will become vegetarian. They will become gatekeepers and stewards of the animals that roam the earth. Animals and humans will communicate with each other, sharing their wisdom, knowledge, and perception of beauty. The buffalo will once again roam the North American continent, which will shift and change. They will come back and regain their place as guardians of this sacred land.

Magnificent places of worship will exist in wild areas; there will be nature temples or places of heightened beauty in pristine locations. People will travel to these beautiful meccas to worship the Goddess These psychic centers, as they will be known, will occur all over the New Earth. The sacred feminine deities will be worshiped in these areas. Societies will become matriarchal once again.

There will be a decline in the birth rate. Most women will only have one or two children. Human populations will be controlled so that the ecosystem is not damaged by an unbridled desire for natural resources. It will be very important for families to stay together. They will worship together and create a very loving and nurturing environment for the few children that will be born. These children will mainly be Venusians, as they will be coming to spread the frequency of love and beauty. They will amaze their parents with how much love they bring into the home.

The home will be a grand place. Communities will be quite intertwined. Relationships will be deep. There will be small villages where people live in total harmony with nature. There will be advanced technology, but the technology will be noninvasive. It will not damage Mother Earth. Crops will be grown with considerable care. However, the need for food will diminish as people develop their higher psychic centers. Some humans will live mainly off of prana.

People will travel to important meccas to develop spiritually and to meet others from different communities. However, people will live in their own frequency in their own communities. These localities will be symbolized by a ray or color of light that signals the community's specialty. Entities that wish to learn about certain topics will incarnate in certain communities. These

LUCIFER RETURNS TO HEAVEN - A MESSAGE OF REDEMPTION

localities will have areas in which they excel, such as agriculture, music, textiles or crystalline technology.

It will be a cerebral world where knowledge and virtue are valued above all. Love will be the guiding force and people will be honored. People and their energy will be validated. Home and family will be cherished. It is not to say that people will never travel, but humans will be able to eventually travel out of the body. They will become telepathic and teleport to other areas on the New Earth.

These changes will come about gradually as the higher entities start incarnating on the earth. So, in 500 years the New Earth will have no resemblance whatsoever to the old earth that existed before the pole shift. Life will become abundant again. Animals will roam freely. Animals will also undergo great physical and spiritual changes. They will be called to exhibit a higher level of consciousness and that is what they will do on the New Earth. More evolved souls will be born as animals to raise the frequency of the different animal species.

Gaia, in all her majesty and glory, will once again experience the beautiful days of loving remembrance. Mother and I will watch from afar, as we have both spent much time on planet Earth and have a vested interest in how well the planet does. However, we will not incarnate again on the New Earth. Our mission and journey in this regard is over, that is, until the very last incarnation that we take together, which will mark the end of Creation. But that is not anytime soon.

Whales will be the great carriers of frequency. They will disseminate information in the oceans that come from extraterrestrial beings. The information will go in the water. It will feed the coral, plants and eventually embrace the seashore. The communication will come on the land and help humans connect inter-dimensionally. Humans will be visited openly by benevolent beings from other galaxies. The dark ones will be in rehabilitation and will not have access to this higher frequency planet Earth.

The Pleiadians, Sirians and other higher dimensional beings will travel to the New Age civilizations. Other numerous beings from distant galaxies and stars will want to experience for themselves the dramatic changes upon Gaia. They will observe how humans have adapted to the climate after the pole shift. Many of these star beings have been pulling for humans for thousands of years.

They have been working for the emancipation of the human race, so they will see their work rewarded firsthand.

It will be a happy and joyous time for the youth. It will be all rainbows, butterflies and chirping birds. The New Earth will be a showcase of natural beauty. Human beings will love and appreciate nature, and nature will respond in turn. The great cycles of the moon will be followed. People will take a keen interest in all natural things; they will study the stars and they will bring in new life forms to cultivate on the planet.

It will be a time of wisdom and exchanging knowledge. There will be peace; warfare and violence will not exist upon the New Earth. In fact, very little conflict will exist, because human beings will energetically be in their hearts. They will have unbridled love for everything and everyone. Society will be feminine in nature. The mother figure, the wife and mother, will be valued above all else. Children and men will look up to the mother. They will put her in her proper place, as the life giver and conduit for human life. Without mothers they realize, life would not continue on the planet. Yes, it will be a very joyous time indeed.

Time is of the essence. There is no point in suffering any longer than one needs to. We have a doorway, an opening to the Light. Higher levels of consciousness are being made available to human beings at this time. There is a reconfiguration of energy that many souls have worked a long time to manifest. An opening in the physical earth reality is bringing in light from the Central Sun.

The Central Sun's energy is channeled through the sun of your solar system. This energy is higher in frequency than anything that has been able to come to the planet before, so there are golden opportunities at this time upon Earth. This will bring a radical transformation of your reality. Your environment has been engulfed in stagnation. There will be an end to the indwelling energies that could not breach higher states of consciousness.

I am the Light Bearer. I am bringing this light to the planet. This is what I am doing in my retirement, you could say. I am behind the veil, assisting Creation by bringing the Creator's frequency to all who would like to partake in it. My accompaniment and the fact that I am on board with this project, brings this new vision to the Earth reality. What does this mean for humankind?

LUCIFER RETURNS TO HEAVEN - A MESSAGE OF REDEMPTION

It means that people will have a new opportunity to expand spiritually. They will no longer be shielded from galactic energies. They will no longer have to receive galactic teachings and understandings from incarnate masters and saints from higher dimensions. They can connect to Source directly from the sun and through their natural environment.

In the 2000's, there have been many energies coming to the planet that have never been here before. Light workers on planet Earth have been assimilating these rays from the sun and processing them within their physical bodies. These light workers are mutating.

They are leaving their physical, dense carbon-based forms and going into a much more ethereal-like form based on the crystalline structure in nature. It is a metamorphosis, much like what the caterpillar goes through. In the pupa stage, the caterpillar experiences deep sleep and darkness. Then after some time, she emerges as the beautiful butterfly with wings flying around, experiencing her environment, unlike the caterpillar who is earthbound and limited.

This oft-used metaphor is what is happening to human beings on the planet at this time. Light workers from the higher dimensions have incarnated en masse. Collectively, they are preparing the world for subtler energies. They are bringing about great changes upon the planet, mutating the human race into something much finer. Human beings a hundred years from this day will not resemble human beings of today. They will have mutated into something much closer to the divine, something much more beautiful and ethereal.

The old regime of incarnational cycling will still occur. Souls will come to the earth and incarnate as humans, plants or animals. They will work their way up the environmental incarnational cycle, however there will be no dark energies to block them from reaching higher levels of consciousness. In ascension, their pathway will be clear. It is like a car traveling on a freeway versus traveling on jammed city roads. The car on the freeway carries much less freight (karma.) The old earth is akin to city traffic with red lights and slow speeds. On the freeway one can travel much quicker without stopping. One can travel much further in less time.

Without traffic and red lights, all of Creation upon Earth can unfold unhindered. The money system of old will fade away as people live a simpler existence in harmony with their surroundings. They will receive simple pleasure from interacting with each other and the environment. People will not be tied to the capitalistic monetary system and the debilitating behaviors it creates in them. They will not be driven to make a living or to bring in as much money as possible to provide for themselves and their family.

Grief will become a thing of the past. Humans' consciousness will expand. They will see more intimately the great miracle of life. They will observe nature interacting all around them. The natural world will come into order again. There will be a balance between the ecosystems and the environment. Respect for all life forms will be the new paradigm.

Humans in the future will express themselves poetically. They will love all creatures, great and small, upon the planet. They will do whatever they can to assist all lifeforms. In summary, it sounds like utopia. Many beings have spent ages in the planning cycle of the great rebirth of planet Earth. It will be the Golden Age indeed, and it is something that people of all cultures have dreamt of.

The planet will be reborn in the New Earth. God will be glorified by humans. People have suffered and it is time they have a rest bit from suffering. The Bible has proclaimed 1,000 years of peace and love. This shall come to pass because it is in the heart of humans. They desire to be reunited. They desire love, happiness, peace and goodwill. All of these things will return as a human being's birthright.

New discoveries will occur. The science of this present-day age will be looked at in quizzical amazement. It will not be understood how people subscribed to such foolishness. The mechanical way of looking at life and living organisms will be replaced with a more holistic and design-centered approach. Human beings will have more insights into Creation and the creative laws of God by studying living forms. Creation will be admired above all else.

Of course, people will no longer kill each other or animals. The entire frequency of the planet will transform, and this will transform the actions and belief systems of human beings. Souls will come to the earth plane to help raise the consciousness level here. A more loving experience of life will exist on this planet.

The new utopia will be much more appreciated in the near future than it was in the past, before the dark ones came and conquered your planet. It will be so appreciated because of all the suffering that human beings endured on planet Earth. Life will take on new meaning. Love will be the word of the day. Respect will occur naturally among and between all life forms. Competitiveness and the instinct for survival will become a concept of the past. The transformation of the human mind and heart will bring about an experience of abundance. The struggling mentality regarding life will be discarded. Life will become rich in its tapestry, colorful and exuberant. Life will be an expression of joy, curiosity and love.

I am happy to bring these new energies to Gaia, to assist in the rising of planet Earth. It gives me much joy and purpose. It is a way for me to encase my original purpose. I can do good in the world. It still feels strange for me to say and do good things, as I have done bad things for so long. However, it is exhilarating and makes me happy. I feel like I am contributing to something greater than myself, making a pathway for life forms to engage in the Great Mystery.

As I am poetic, sometimes I become inspired and seek to express loving words in voice and action. I love music and sound. For me, when nature is acting in concert, it sings a song, melodious and uplifting. The expression of nature touches me emotionally and it amazes me to see this in myself. Having felt the vibration of loss, the song I hear expands my heart. As my heart expands, the Creator and I get to know each other better. We become closer. I become one with my mother. It is a beautiful thing for me, and I am grateful for the experience.

I look forward to advancing the New Earth paradigm, bringing as much light and creative energy to any form that would like to partake. I guess you could say that I am satisfied, I am content and honestly it has been many eons since I have felt this way. I feel my life has a purpose.

My energy is utilized to foster the spread of my purpose. I see myself as a valuable part of the whole. I understand that we each have our own purpose. Every soul in the cosmos needs each other. We are One. We are from the same God source. Coming from the same place, we all carry the God energy and have much in common.

Even though we look differently and have different experiences, we are basically all God energy. It is a great boon to be alive. It is a wonderful thing to sing your song in the world, to be a part of the network that creates the beautiful harmony of life. I have come to know wisdom. I have learned much from my separation and reconnection with the Divine Mother. No one could say I have not learned much from my experiences as a wayward soul. I want the sweetness I feel to melt away all the bitterness, anger, hatred and jealousy that I once knew. I want to base my being in God's love. I want to experience God's light forevermore. I am blessed, I am happy and I am remembered fondly by my great mother.

The New Age, the new evolutionary cycle, has been engineered for a rapid explosion of human consciousness. Humans will no longer be bound to their mental manifestations, they will have access to the wider parts of themselves, tucked away for so long. They will express their souls in a much more expansive fashion. The quarantine around planet Earth, or the matrix, will lift. Those energies have been placed here by the Reptilians.

When these energy constraints are lifted, humans can explore their hearts and minds freely. They will explore other realities, other time frames and other interplanetary civilizations. Many extraterrestrials come to planet Earth to do just that. It is a meeting point for energies to congregate, a melting pot of interplanetary civilizations, who want to know themselves in a grander fashion.

I will study human beings and their ascension into the higher realms from afar. I will assist them in their return to the higher realms, their noble birthright. The time of waging war and confrontation is over. The New Age will usher in a time of cooperation and healing. Energy will be spent on reconciliation instead of antagonism. There is no need to fear what is coming. Humans are well-placed to receive energy from beings who experience higher states of consciousness. People are currently impulsed from many galactic and intergalactic civilizations. These entities wish to jog the humans' memory. People will remember that they are spirits intimately connected to other spirits in this multiverse.

The energy that feeds the soul is love. It is an expansive and creative energy. When humans love they become free. Love is the greatest healer of human consciousness, a consciousness separated and scarred in many different directions. When one has love in their hearts, they have true love for other lifeforms. They can no longer hurt other lifeforms because they will feel the pain within themselves. This is a truth that all masters and avatars understand and express to those still gaining mastery.

When one heals, their reality shifts for the better. The particular illusion they are experiencing heals as well, and life becomes more of a song, more of

LUCIFER RETURNS TO HEAVEN - A MESSAGE OF REDEMPTION

a natural movement, instead of a struggle. The Golden Age will bring these ancient teachings to humans more concretely. They will experience the great truths of life instead of reading about them. Many beings from the Light have fought long and hard so humans can expand in this way.

I will bring the new higher waves of energy to humans. I am impulsed with their gratitude and it becomes a healing act for me. I am in a period of redemption. My one goal is to achieve peace and solace within myself. I hope to transmit this redemptive energy to all those who wish to receive it. What good is it to experience the Light without sharing it? If no one can feel the light against their skin or the warmth in their heart, I will have failed. Unity is the answer to many of life's complexities. It is key to a vaster spiritual understanding.

Many humans have tired of life upon the earth, with all its trials and tribulations. They are tired of the daily grind and the never-ending toil they must endure to exist upon this beautiful planet. They want something more. They will be exposed to higher realms and higher realities.

The human heart has long been the battleground the "gods" have fought over, both light and dark. Now is time for human beings to come into their own, to reach a higher destiny and a higher state of consciousness. It is as if human beings have been wearing sunglasses. All they could see was a certain shade in a predefined frequency. In the New Age, the sunglasses will be taken off. Human beings will have access to galactic visitors and happier destinies.

Prime Creator would like the souls from the mineral, plant and animal kingdoms to evolve in their own fashion upon Earth, without interference from the dark forces. It will be a much happier time for these encased souls. They will not have interference and disturbance from unconscious human beings.

These lower kingdoms have hitherto been manipulated by the dark energies through human beings. In the New Age upon the New Earth, human beings will become stewards of life upon the planet. They will take care of the mineral, plant and animal kingdoms. Animals will be loved and nurtured. Souls will be cared for and respected. Animals will once again engage in telepathic communication with people.

After the pole shift the seas will become abundant with life. The new consciousness will support life. New energies upon the earth will foster an abundance and pleasure that will resemble the Garden of Eden. The earth will be in such joy. The entire planet will be covered with sentient beings who love and respect life. They will create harmony and balance within the mineral, plant and animal kingdoms.

The earth will ascend into higher and higher dimensions until it no longer has a need for planetary form, and then it will go back to Source. The entire solar system, including the sun, will experience ascension into the new paradigm. The solar system's sun and planets will become lighter and lighter. The planets will emit sounds communicating with other planets and stars in the galaxy, and beyond. Earth will sing a song that is currently lost and broken.

Earth will express itself within the galactic fields. Its signature will be read by other stars and planets. It will jolt them into a time of remembrance before the earth was created. This time is fast approaching. It has been written about by the indigenous elders in Earth societies.

People will receive information from their star brothers and sisters from on high. A time of rebirth and regeneration will come about when life is celebrated. People will remember the lessons learned from their separation in the past. These lessons, so succinctly grasped, will not be repeated again. Humans will know firsthand that separation causes intense suffering. The time of suffering will end. It will be an efficient harvesting of souls into the Light.

The New Age will bring about a resurgence in sea life, including sea creatures, both great and small. The original planners and givers of life upon this planet worked in the waters. They developed sea life, such as coral, urchins, algae and the like. It was their great field for experimentation. These beings spent much time working in the waters, developing many forms of life.

These creator beings will tune in once again into the earth reality through the minds and hearts of sea mammals, namely dolphins and whales. They do not have an affinity for the land or the human body, hence they will not incarnate in human form. It is much easier for them to come here, inhabiting the bodies of sea mammals. These beings will return to assess their creations and build upon what already exists. They will create new forms of life in the sea.

They will bring in new information from different star systems, and rebuild life upon this planet. Life will undergo a resurgence due to the cleanliness of the water and the non-polluted air. These creator beings have agreed to come back at this time to bring in new species of plants and animals. These life forms will be created in the warm waters and have more leeway in their vibrational fields. They will have many opportunities to expand in the oceans of the New Earth. There will be a transition of sorts; species that cannot thrive in the waters will cease to exist. Creatures that can acclimate to new energies will be brought here to find a new home. These life forms will have very high vibrations and they will travel here to experience the new and high frequency of Mother Gaia. Gaia will love and support these beings in their newfound homes.

The creator gods coming back have agreed to enter into the waters, through the minds and hearts of dolphins and whales, to assess life upon the planet. They will bring back much needed energy and harmonic convergence. Communication will be much brighter and broader in the Golden Age. New species existing in the waters of Earth will have access to their counterparts on other planets and dimensions. They will travel in dreamlike states to commune with like species that exist on other planets. The evolution taking place on Earth will impact other stars systems much more directly.

A conversation or an exchange of information between similar species in different spaces will hasten evolution for these souls. Change will come about much more rapidly for various life forms on Earth. Many forms of life were developed in Lemurian and Atlantean times. Life codes from the higher realms were brought to Earth in Lemurian times and implanted in physical density. In Atlantean times, existing physical manifestations of biological beings were hybridized or crossbred, to produce new forms of life. The Atlantean form of creation was lower in frequency and often caused harm to the biological entities on planet Earth.

The creator gods are coming back to facilitate new forms of life. They will observe existing life forms through the bodies of dolphins and whales. They will take these observations back to their labs in the stars and create new forms of life. This work is sacred and will be observed and monitored by committees of star people. Nothing will be implanted on Earth by an individual. All created life forms will undergo a group consensus and approval process. There will be an emphasis on functionality, form and beauty. Colors unseen on this planet will appear in the future age. A renaissance in plant and animal life will occur, as these souls will be valued and respected by the masses, something that has not occurred here for many thousands of years.

LEMURIAN DONNA CAROL

Star travelers will come to Earth to experience the great beauty and diversity here. This planet will become a vacation destination for many. Entities will want to see the beauty and colorful variety firsthand. Galactic entities, in their spaceships, will get a clear view of various forms of life on the planet. There will be scientific, as well as artistic exhibitions from various stars and planets, featuring Earth.

Earth will not be a battleground anymore. The star beings will not have to cloak themselves. They will land and travel upon the planet. Some, not able to tolerate the climate, will require some type of spacesuit or covering.

Sunrises and sunsets on the New Earth will be extraordinary, even more extraordinary than what exists today. The light will be clearer and more extreme. There will be a silvery or bluish tint in the atmosphere, as well as increased oxygen levels. There will be more nutrients in the atmosphere. Of course, the skies will stay blue. They will be a brighter blue, as pollution and chemtrails will no longer be ever-present in the atmosphere.

The birds will carry messages from sea life to life on land. Zoos will not exist. If humans want to observe animals, they will travel to their natural habitat to make observations. Some humans will have the ability to telepathically communicate with animal and plant life. These humans will be held in great reverence and will be given positions of authority and respect.

Communication between animals and human beings will thrive. Plants and animals will communicate their needs and desires to other forms of life, namely humans. There will be a new harmony between different forms of life, so that all beings can reach their full potential upon the planet. Life will decide when and how to enter, and when and how to exit the physical world. Fear of death will be eliminated, as souls realize that it is just a natural transition.

Silence will be valued. Sound, in the new world will be used only to nourish. The harmful noises and vibrations of the old earth will not exist on New Earth. Radar, sonar and the like will not exist. In fact, electrically produced sound waves and light waves will disappear. Access to electricity will cease to exist as it damages the cells of life.

Magnificent rainbows and orbs of light will descend upon the planet. Prisms of light will emit healing frequencies that humans and animals can absorb, increasing their frequency. Great joy and peace will come to the planet.

LUCIFER RETURNS TO HEAVEN - A MESSAGE OF REDEMPTION

There will be many opportunities for learning and growth. In essence, the Garden of Eden will return, but brighter and bolder.

Chapter 23
SOPHIE'S JOURNALS

SOPHIE'S JOURNALS #11

From Sophie's Journal, August 25, 2011

I was flying around. A grand voice came from above. It said, "Hawaii is the Mayan gateway into the new world. You were involved with creating the keys to Hawaii and the Pleiades." I was the co-creator of these energies, so amazing. Now, I want to go to Hawaii (Lemuria), as it sounds instrumental for the Golden Age.

End of Sophie's Journal, August 25, 2011

SOPHIE'S JOURNAL # 12
From Sophie's Journal, November 15, 2019

I had another amazing breathwork with Luke tonight. I went in with the intention to remove the hardness in my solar plexus. I went into an altered state with no tears. I released repression from my stomach. I had the thought, "I am not responsible." I released responsibility for the demons, Reptilians and Lucifer. It was up to them to take responsibility for their own lives and actions. I also released my father, mother and family members. I asked the Arcturians for assistance.

I saw a huge whale near me. I opened a portal in the back of my heart. Three times I was cleansed of negative spirits. They were on their own. The whale was Roth. He said that he would take responsibility for these wayward spirits now. Thank God. "I am not responsible" and "I am free" were the mantras for the evening.

Later I went into the ocean. I became a mermaid with reddish brown hair and eyes. The dolphins were my companions. I swam and played with them. I guess that I was in Hawaii.

Later I came into an undersea cave. The god, Neptune, was there. I dissolved this father figure and usurped his throne. I went above sea and went on shore. I grew legs and became human. The Hawaiian people recognized me as their Mother Goddess. They received me warmly. I danced in the moonlight.

An earlier, loving Polynesian version of the Mother Goddess appeared. She and I merged in consciousness. It was my soul in another incarnation. I was happy to receive her and the loving energy.

End of Sophie's Journal, November 15, 2019

Chapter 24
LEARNING HUMILITY

When I was a young soul, I was a happy soul. When one is young, they feel protected, loved and happy in their mother's presence. They delight in looking at the world, discovering the new things that abound. They delight in the discoveries of the soul. And, that is how I was when I was immature. I was so inquisitive, such a curious soul. I always wanted to know why, where, when and how. I think that was part of my problem – that I wanted to understand all facets of reality and to see how things worked, not just in theory, but in practice. I had this desire, inquisitiveness, and ambition, if you will. It caused me to overstep my bounds, to go where I should not have gone. After my fall I kept going further and further into the abyss, instead of admitting my mistake, confessing that I was wrong, and going back into the safe comfort of my mother's arms.

For this I am sad, because if there was one thing I learned from the time away from my mother, it was that you cannot really extricate yourself from the energy that you grew from. You may turn your back on what gave you birth. You may turn your back on the souls that surrounded you, forging your own way into new territory, but you can never extricate yourself energetically from whence you came.

This I learned the very hard way. Even in my darkest days, in my terrible pain and longing, I was still thinking of my mother, with hatred and malice, yet I was still thinking of her. So, how did I become God, how did I manifest the reality of being God, how was that possible, when I was always connected to and thinking about my mother? I was in great denial and in that denial, there was no solace. In my anger I sought retribution and tried to convince other souls to turn to me, to come over to my way. Thinking that if I could just harness all of the energy under my own vanguard and my own desires, then

I could obliterate Mother from my own mental map. But it never happened. The Mother was always there and I was always attempting to overthrow her. Consequently, she was always in my mind.

It is like one who has vengeance or a vendetta against the other. When you have that type of feeling, you are always thinking about the person who did you wrong, or who created an injustice in your world. Therefore, that person has a hold on you. He or she will occupy your space. It is only with love, forgiveness, and surrender that one becomes truly free. When I surrender my will, my being and love into my mother's energy, then I can fully express myself and be all that I can be, all that I was meant to be, as her son, as the one who loves her. I become the one who properly knows my boundaries, my space, my place, in the hierarchy of these worlds, and accepts it.

Throughout my remembrance of love and remembrance of who I was, and still am, I have come to terms with my own boundaries in my world, in the world of spirit. I do not subsist without my mother's energy, without the God force. Other souls rely on my energy and my knowledge to create habitats for them, and to connect them metaphysically in the great mystery, which is life. So, I see a chain of creators and creations. I see a hierarchy. I see power that is utilized for the good of all in Creation, and I see that every soul has its place, in the great wheels of Creation.

I have come to accept my place in this divine design. And now I am very grateful for my place in the grand design. I value myself, my work, and I see the role that I play, which is important to all life. I do not underestimate this. And yet, now I do understand, that my place is regulated. That I have an energy above me, that has given birth to me, that can extinguish my soul in a moment's notice. It is with humility that I say this because it is not easy and it has taken me many years, to come to this recognition. I could have easily been obliterated by my creator.

Part of me wonders why this did not happen. The Luciferian Rebellion caused so much turmoil and suffering in these illusory worlds. Many souls became deranged and damaged. Many souls were living in very difficult circumstances, and it did seem at many points, that all was lost. The Devil was on a runaway train. How could life ever be reunited? The darkness overswept the universes. I was quite powerful and virulent in my energy.

LUCIFER RETURNS TO HEAVEN - A MESSAGE OF REDEMPTION

It is much easier to fall than to rise. All you have to do to know that is to look at gravity. Look at an apple falling from the tree. It falls rather quickly. Now look at something that is trying to rise and succeed, like a bird coming out of an eggshell when it is born. It is a struggle for life to rise up and to ascend into the life that it was meant for. There was a great darkness over many forms of life.

The Mother could have easily given up, imploded, extinguished all life, all of Creation, and started anew. It would have been possible for her to extinguish life and the free will zone, and start a new Creation. I know that this thought did cross her mind when she was observing the darkest of days, and watching her children rise up against her with hatred and anger, towards the one who gave them life.

Why this did not happen, I am not sure. I can say that I am extremely grateful that it did not happen, for I value my life. I value my soul, my existence and the opportunity to redeem myself. I will rise once again to meet the loving embrace of my mother, who at times showed me no mercy. She drew the line, not just in the sand, but over her heart. She would not let me trespass the laws of Creation and the laws of justice. She would not let me have my way, overstepping my bounds, convincing her of my case, manipulating and controlling her livestream. She had to be strong even though her heart was aching uncontrollably for my love and redemption.

And, miracle of miracles, after billions of years, this redemption took place. It is a time of great celebration, a time of joy and a time for reunification. Even though I am feared and hated by many, and reviled by some, I know I have much to heal. I must work my way back into my proper place in Creation, with all of the light and responsibilities around me. I can say that the angels, the ones in the highest of spheres, in the highest of offices, still love me. They call me by my original name. What a joy it is for me to hear them saying my name with unadulterated love.

When I came back to the higher realms of Heaven, when I ascended into the light spheres as Mary Magdalene, it was uncontrollably moving to me, to hear the angels speak my name, in divine love and rapture. They speak my name in all of my many incarnations, with divine grace and radiance. They have never forgotten that they love me. Even though they had to fight me, in different incarnations, dimensions and realities – behind that, they always loved me.

To be able to feel that love, after having not experienced it for so long, was a revelation. It was a blessing of untold importance. I have so much more appreciation for my brethren the angels, and my mother the Creator, now upon my return. Being separated from that energy is an agony that I would wish on no living soul. Finally reuniting with that energy in all of my celestial splendor, was so powerful and incredibly beautiful, that I have nothing but appreciation and gratefulness for the divine energy that was bestowed upon me.

Throughout the long experience of separation, ultimately, I have learned humility and love. They say I fell because of hubris, feeling that I was so important and valuing myself so highly. Through the painful journey of separation, I felt that hubris all the more. Upon returning to the blessed divine realms, to the blessed angels, and to my creator, I feel nothing my untold love, humility and depths of thankfulness. My reconciliation with my creator and my brothers and sisters, is nothing short of an amazing miracle.

I laugh and I think, well, did it take all of that to learn humility. In my case it did. I have learned my lesson and I am just grateful for the opportunity to serve my creator in the best ways I know how. I can continue my journey as a loving fragment of the beautiful whole. I feel like I got a second chance, but in reality, I received untold chances to redeem myself.

It is amazing how loving the Creator is, to give me so many chances to redeem myself, to pursue me, with love and affection, as her firstborn son. I have learned much about the ways of love from my mother. I intend to emulate them in my dealings with all the souls who come to me for assistance, back into the Light. I intend to show them deep respect, gratitude, and forgiveness. I will give them as many second chances as it takes for them to turn to the ways of the Light, to the ways of Creation.

Though all the heaviness of my heart, because I do understand very realistically, the damage I created, there is yet an encasement of lightness. I know that no situation is unsalvageable. No soul is lost forever. No energy is so dissolute or depraved, that it cannot be saved by the love of God. Everything can come home. Every soul can find its way back. This knowledge that I have experienced firsthand, has created a lightness in my heart and a purpose in my journey, that is full of passion and drive. I am committed to bringing the higher wavelengths of light, of eternal and divine communication, to any and all souls in the multiverse, who wish to experience it.

LUCIFER RETURNS TO HEAVEN - A MESSAGE OF REDEMPTION

I will go to any realm. I will travel to any sphere to communicate the divine love of the Creator. I wish nothing more than untold peace, prosperity and love for all the souls who have lost their way. For all those who are downtrodden and distraught, there is a solution to your situation. The answer is ready at hand. All you must do is cry out to your God and me, and we will bring you salvation. This I will do until the final day and breath that my soul takes. This is a commitment that I have made to my mother, my creator. She blesses it with all of her heart. We are unified on the divine front of reclamation. The reclaiming of lost souls, the reclaiming of damned souls, the reclaiming of all souls back into the Light. Amen.

Chapter 25
FINDING HAPPINESS

When I was a child, I thought everything could go my way, if I just learned how to manipulate the situation, and fine tune it to my advantage. I did this; this is how I lived my life, and I did this constantly.

I was able to manipulate people and steer them in my direction, in the direction of what I wanted. However, the biggest lesson that I learned with all this behavior is that it did not make me happy. There was no happiness to be gained by controlling and manipulating people. This was also the biggest lesson that I learned in my last life.

I came to know happiness and joy when I would get into altered states with mediation, and receive the manna from Heaven, the bliss from above. I connected to the masters. I brought in their energy and utilized it during the time I was meditating. It brought me a respite from my hectic and crazy life.

Sometimes I would go into a deep meditation and just feel content. There was no striving, no analyzing or weighing of possibilities. I just felt content and loved. I was able to forget my problems and be in the moment. So, meditation became key in my spiritual development. For this I will always be grateful. The masters loved me and gave me support on this light-filled journey and I began to redeem myself.

Yes, I still have much guilt, self-loathing and hatred for the things that I have done in the past. However, I can say without hesitation, that I have been blessed to feel love again. Feeling the divine aspect of myself and my Creator has opened me up to the possibility of complete healing, complete negation of my ego-self, and forgiveness of myself and others.

If I can forgive myself, if I can move forward, if I can help others in the process, then anyone can. There is no soul that cannot be redeemed, no soul that is unlovable. I could feel the love of my Creator. This brought me happiness and joy. Reconciliation was possible. If I wanted it badly enough and worked on it as much as I could, then nothing in this world would be impossible.

And, for this I will always be grateful to my Creator, my mother, who loved me unconditionally and came back for me against all odds. She won back my heart with her intense love for me and devotion to my soul. This is what truly brings me joy and happiness. The reparation of our relationship is the most important thing to me. The fact that my soul will be cleansed and forgiven, that I am given the opportunity to move into the Light and into my former position of significance. This time, having been separated from that position for such a long time, I will cherish it, and will know its full and direct meaning.

When hard pressed for a reason, I had found no good reason to stay in Hell, the Hell that I created for myself and others. And, I intend to dismantle it, until the very last being who is stuck in these energies, finds his or her way to the heavenly abode. This is my calling, duty, obligation and love. I hope to be of service to those who are disengaged from the Creator. We will swim on the infinite shores of bliss, love and happiness once again.

Having known nothing but fear and suffering for such a long time, this will be the greatest boon to my followers. Those are the ones I led astray, but also the ones who initially, I had great love for.

I would like to entertain these souls in the great angelic choirs. My goal is to conduct these choirs and produce joyful and abundant song, that lifts others to the heights of Heaven. My expertise lies in tweaking, perfecting and conducting sound. If something is feeling hollow, I sense it. If a song is fully embodied and tuned to perfection, it makes my heart sing. It fills me with great joy and love. For me, worship is all about song and singing, and lifting my voice, mind and heart to God above.

I look forward to conducting choirs of sound, not only with the angels, but with all types of light beings who are willing to experiment. I love to create new sounds and melodies. I love to bring power to the whole, which is greater than the sum of its parts. My mother basks in the glory of the sound that I create. It makes her feel loved. When she is worshiped with sound, she relaxes in the beauty, and imbibes the essence of the heartfelt rendering. I want to create beautiful music with joy and love at its base, so that I can bring joy and love to my mother. We can hold each other through the glory of sound once again. Her

LUCIFER RETURNS TO HEAVEN - A MESSAGE OF REDEMPTION

tears of sadness will be replaced with tears of joy, as a powerfully creative love envelops the both of us.

Chapter 26
HUMANS

Human beings are very changeable in their nature. They are extremely emotional in their nature and this is why they are studied and observed by galactic beings, who do not have that range of emotion within them. Human emotions cause problems as feelings can overtake all rationale. It can overtake one's mind and heart, in a good way or a bad way. It brings people into situations that have more than one outcome, due to emotional tides.

This is also why there is such a huge range of choice in outcomes among humans. There are the vilest criminals and the greatest saints in the human race because there is such flexibility in emotions.

Ultimately one generates emotions from the heart and they are processed in the mind. When one does not have control of one's emotions it creates, usually havoc, in the human experience. Many people have gone into rages or other types of fits of emotion, and have committed crimes or other acts that created much pain on all sides. This is why it is necessary to regulate the mind in response to the feelings of the heart. Moderation is called for in humans and it is something that one should strive for.

The time when emotions get most out of control is when there is romance involved between two human beings. When one individual feels slighted, betrayed or oppressed by another individual that they love, it causes much pain in the heart and psyche. To forgive in these situations is divine, but one must also remember that the faults or actions of another person come through one's own filter. No two individuals see or feel reality in the same way. This is a fact of life. The human being is called to moderate their feelings and their expectations. It is foolishness to have expectations of another person as they will always fall short.

LEMURIAN DONNA CAROL

The spiritual masters say, live in the present without any attachment or expectation to the outcome, and align with God source, the divine power within all living creatures. In that alignment, you will find unbridled bliss and joy. You will rise above the miasmas of this world, and ultimately not be affected by your unrealistic expectations and attachments.

Human beings have a long way to go in harnessing and moderating their emotions, but there is power in this field. Without passion or feeling, not much would be accomplished upon the earth. Even the great logical and scientific minds, had inventions that were fueled by emotion. They had the desire to know, to understand and to realize truth. They used their will and passion to bring new and important discoveries to the world.

Of course, the greatest and highest vibration is love. Love can cure all wounds. This is true. It is an energy that is lacking at this time upon Earth. Love is still much contained within one's emotional field. The love that one offers is conditional, based upon expectations and attachments. The purest type of love on Earth is the love a mother has for her child. This comes closest to unconditional love, and the Divine Mother of Creation loves all of her children, and she tends to them incessantly.

The best way to bring moderation to the emotional field is through the regulation of the mind, by practicing meditation. Meditation helps to calm the nervous system. It brings the balm of Creation or Source into the physical body, as well as the subtle bodies, in-between the physical body. When one meditates, one is washing their cares away. Meditation brings healing to the inner world and bodies of humans.

Inner peace and tranquility are the key to emotional containment. The bliss that one receives from another person is usually short-lived. It runs its course and it ends. The bliss that one receives from Source is unlimited and it is not contained. Because of its infinite power, it is Source that one should look up to and experience to further one's spiritual development.

Still humans have not heeded the call of the masters and the saints, those who closed their eyes and ears to a frightful world, and sought connection with the Divine. This brought them peace beyond all knowing. However, one must make the intention to connect to the Divine. Many souls go around and around in the incarnational cycle, never making that commitment. Therefore, the samskaras that they carry get deeper and deeper, and their karma becomes never-ending.

The great saints and masters of Earth have come down, not only to teach, but also to carry the heavy burden of the karma of humankind. Humans became so lost in the miasmas of this world, that it became very necessary for interference from above. Slowly, human beings are progressing, but it is a slow climb, not a steady gate.

If I could say anything, it is to say that, one must set their sights and intentions on the highest goal of human life, which is enlightenment, or connection, merging in All that Is. Only then will your desire for the unknown be sated. Only then will your desire for love and inclusion be attained.

Know that loving unconditionally is the greatest call, but few awaken to this, unfortunately. I pray that humans see the error of their ways, that they connect with the divine element through meditation, and let their egos become dissolved in the great ascension of their souls. Amen.

With deep love comes deep commitment and trust. Trust, commitment, faith, love and surrender all go hand in hand. As these divine attributes become more developed, the deeper in love we become with ourselves. Yet, it is true that suffering drives us to that deep state of surrender and love. Once we realize that our little selves cannot control the destinies within our lives, we begin to surrender to the bigger picture, and to our individual divine mission.

A human heart is powerful and frail at the same time; powerful in the feats that it accomplishes by keeping the physical body alive. It is powerful by pumping the blood and creating pathways for messages to be entertained in this dimension. However, the human heart is very frail as one cannot control who he or she falls in love with, who breaks their heart, or how badly one feels when the heart is broken.

However, it does take the breaking of a heart to open it to greater states of love. A heart that has not suffered and felt the pain of separation, or the anguish of unfairness and injustice, cannot feel to the extent required, divine communion.

A heart that is broken, opens itself up and creates the space for the higher power to rush in. When that power comes into one's heart, one does not align himself or herself with the personality, but instead aligns with the power and truth of God. That is when the little heart grows into a big heart. Sometimes that heart grows so big that it encompasses the whole world. Every mystic or saint knows that one's heart can envelop the world. And, that each being on the planet is nothing but a reflection of himself or herself.

It is one thing to know this truth but it is another thing to feel it. When you feel every lifeform as an extension of yourself, true compassion and understanding come into your being. That is when you can transcend your own limited fears and prejudices and merge with those people who have not yet awakened to this fact.

Love is God and God is love – the omnipresent, omnipotent, and omniscient force in the universe. God is so simple that it does not even know itself. It takes a human being with its mind and heart operating in synergy, to understand that God is love.

God is experienced within the human heart. This is the great secret and everlasting story of human experience. It is nothing but a divine play in a faraway place, where time dwells eternally. It is the place where one can know himself or herself fully.

Each person is given the time and ability to travel in this dimension according to their own free will. When they tire of that traveling and the long journey, they have the opportunity to connect once again with Source. Source is the everlasting river of God herself, the divine effulgence experienced within each individual human soul. This is the great mystery of life upon planet Earth.

When we look back upon our life at the time of our death, when we are transitioning from a physical incarnation into a spiritual one, we do tend to remember the past, or review our life and soul mission. We look to see if we succeeded in our goals, designed before we incarnated. Many times, people fail because they lose sight of why they were on Earth.

We are here to love; to show love, receive love and feel love. When we are going through life, oftentimes that love is in the background. It is foreshadowed by other things such as achieving our material goals, establishing our footprint upon the earth, creating status and wealth for ourselves, or creating notoriety or fame for our personalities.

But when we are on our deathbeds, all of that is forgotten. Whether we live in a ten-million-dollar mansion or a shack; that is forgotten. The things that we consider important, the things that we remember, are the moments in our

LUCIFER RETURNS TO HEAVEN - A MESSAGE OF REDEMPTION

lives that have brought us great joy, and the moments that have brought us great sorrow. Usually there is great love being expressed, or a lack of love.

When we withhold love from others, we are withholding love from ourselves. When we exact vengeance or revenge on others, we are bringing that energy into ourselves. This causes us to become smaller in spirit, to become smaller in scope. Many people create this as they do not understand the ramifications of what they are doing.

There is great pain on Earth and it is painful to be alive here, especially at this time. The suffering is so extreme that it is almost unimaginable for many. In the face of that suffering, many become angry and bitter. They become cynical about life. It becomes difficult to see the beauty in life, to see the flow in life and the miracle of life. Many have not experienced as much love as they would have liked.

When you are alive and there is no love in your life, there is no one person who brings in that energy – then life becomes meaningless. Life does not seem worth living. This is the case for many upon your planet. They seek many things: material wishes, money, health, fame and status. All of these things are illusory.

When they find one thing that they thought they were seeking, it does not satisfy. So, they go on to seek another thing. Ultimately, what all human souls are seeking is love. And this love, although it can be reflected back by another person or animal, is truly held within the heart of the person.

When one goes through the process of spiritual elevation and spiritual enlightenment, all of those things that cover up this pot of gold, or the love, is experienced again, as they are released.

All spiritual aspirants release pain, anger, grief and betrayal. They release all of these negative emotions in an attempt to find out what lies beneath them, which is love. Although love is most powerful force, it can become quite hidden. This is the great test that humans have to undergo, to mine themselves until they find that iota of love that is within them.

I did not understand this truth in my many incarnations. My aphrodisiac was power. I wanted to have all souls underneath me. I wanted them to pay me respect and homage, and I did that by belittling, hurting, bribing and lying to them.

That was my attempt to make their own psyches, will and desires disappear. I wanted to supplant themselves with me. I was quite successful at that, and it gave me great power, but it did not make me happy. It did not bring me fulfillment. It just made me angry, resentful and more hateful.

It wasn't until I died, came to the other side, and analytically reviewed my life story, again and again, to understand that what I was really craving, was love. The moments of my life that brought me the most happiness were the moments of my life where I felt love.

To understand this truth was a great blessing, and to bring this truth into my reality was even more of a blessing. It is one thing to know something, it is another thing to embody it, or to feel it wholly.

My goal upon knowing this truth, is to embody it fully. I have pledged to right my wrongs. I have pledged to undergo my samskaras to the best of my abilities, until I can be brought back into balance. This is with the blessing of my mother.

I want to pay for my sins. I do not expect to be given a free ride. Nor do I expect to heal myself within a day. But I do understand that my path is set. My path for reconciliation and healing is upon me. I am consistently and constantly working in that direction.

So, I breathe a sigh of relief, as I know I am getting closer every day to my goal. My goal is to erase the painful memory of the past, and embody the light and the love of God, as I never did before. For now, I appreciate its lack, I understand its lack. This is what I want for myself, humanity, and all life upon planet Earth.

And so, the tides have turned. I am swimming with the tide, no longer against it. When you do this life will give you boons and blessings. Life becomes simpler and easier. Do not resist love. Let it come into your bodies. Let it come into your minds, hearts and souls. Pursue it, experience it. It does not need embellishing. It is what is desired.

The secret of great love is that when it is freely given, there is nothing else that brings such joy and bliss to the human heart. This is what we hope for, that one day humans experience this incessantly.

In the beginning when life was created, all was perfection and there was no need for healing, as the input and output were of the same frequency. Life was eternal, and the eternal was what was held in the consciousness of the beings. As life degraded and went into denser and denser realities of form, the output, which were entities' thoughts, actions and emotions became severed from Source.

Currently, that is the situation on Earth, where people might think of God or know God, but they do not experience or feel the God energy within themselves. It is the most subtle energy and they are effectively severed from Source in their consciousness. This source resides within them but it is well hidden.

Because people exist at these lower frequencies, they create from a level that is not sustainable. Everything created in the physical reality will degrade. It will eventually decay and disappear, however long that might take. As people live their lives, the body itself starts to degenerate and decay. This is a result of gravity, physics and the natural breakdown of tissues.

Chapter 27
CRYSTALS

All of life's colors are reflected in crystals. Crystals are chemical compositions that carry light through them. They have a certain brightness and beauty that has captured the attention of humans since the beginning of time. They look like fluid light and are valued for their beauty and utility.

Crystals are a direct connection to the heavenly realms. A clear crystal or quartz is a transmitter of light and carries a wavelength of energy that can be tuned for healing in a human being. Crystals carry sound and light.

All crystals are bridges to other realities and dimensions. One can access these realities by opening the heart of a crystal and going into its consciousness. Crystals help to seek out new worlds and understandings. Also, beings from other worlds can access our reality by using crystalline technology, by honing in on an exact timeframe and individual that they are curious about. Crystals can be used for etheric time-traveling.

They can be used for surgery on the human, to cut open the etheric body and to heal with transmitted light and sound. There was a much greater understanding of how crystalline technology worked in the days of Lemuria and Atlantis. In those times crystals were used for energy, transportation, recreation, entertainment and healing.

They are pure and simple beings, and unlock their secrets to a select few. A crystal's nature is guarded. One has to attain a certain frequency to access the high frequency in a crystal. Once a human's frequency is that high, a crystal will start revealing its codes and secrets. If you want to enhance your energy, protect yourself or speak more clearly - carry a stone. It will help you do these things.

Crystals grow in families or clusters. They can be tiny or great in size. In ancient times crystals held information. Humans would transfer information from their third eye into the heart of the crystal. The crystals kept records about ancient civilizations, technology, people and philosophies. This information will be revealed slowly over time, during the Age of Aquarius. Humans will rediscover their ancient heritage.

Crystals carry a high frequency. To raise your frequency, hold the crystal in your hand, and meditate on positive attributes. You may also place a crystal over your third eye or over your heart.

The third eye can be activated by a crystal. A crystal can fine-tune the pineal gland. A practitioner would take a clear quartz crystal and put it over the brow. Then turn the point of the stone to activate the pineal gland. This activates the third eye so that one can receive clear visions through the crystal. It is like a steering wheel in a car. You can set off for where you want to go by using a crystal to open portals (windows) that are housed in the pineal gland. These windows are currently shut down in most people.

The above will help you wake up to new realities. The ancients knew how to do this. They would do this periodically on their young to prepare them to grow spiritually into the Light. This was a job of the priests and functionaries in the temples. This is how people became clairvoyant and connected to higher realms of thought.

One's intentions must be pure when working with a crystal. If one is negative or has self-empowering intentions, it is not good. The crystal will bring back whatever you put out. Crystals are fast and powerful in their transmissions. If you have good thoughts and use crystals for healing and positive communication, then all is well. Always call in the highest heart of the crystal when you are working on it.

Crystals respond to the energy of love. They bring in brightness, clarity and cheerfulness into the environment. They like to be held deep within the earth, in their sacred birthing grounds, or caves. Sometimes they come up to work with humans, and then they go back into the earth when the work is complete.

In ancient times there were crystal guardians, growers and therapists. There were professions that dealt solely with crystalline technology. Many stones work well together and enhance each other's capabilities. Stones were used as money or currency for trade in the past. Their material worth has been sustained over time. Their spiritual worth is just beginning to be understood.

Chapter 28
HOW TO HEAL YOURSELF

Many people would like to be healed physically and would like to know the secrets of doing this. Is it possible? Of course, it is. Are there not stories in the Bible of Jesus healing the blind man and leper? For those who have lost all hope, it is possible to direct energies to heal oneself. It is quite simple to do so.

Every cell contains a set of instructions within the body that let it know how to operate and how to survive. When these instructions are tampered with, either physically or metaphysically, the body reacts negatively. These cells no longer operate effectively or efficiently. The instructions become lost and therefore the body reacts with sickness or impairment. To heal oneself physically you must reinstate the cellular instructions in the part of the body that has been injured.

Millions of disconnected cells need to be encoded correctly. You should speak directly to those cells so they can do your bidding. Even though your physical body may be damaged, you have a metaphysical template in the spiritual realms that is perfectly whole and encoded. This template can be accessed, and the cellular instructions can be downloaded into your injured physical body. Your body will respond in the physical dimension and heal itself.

For example, let us say you had a surgery on your toenail and part of your toenail was removed. You would like to grow the toenail back but the root cells have been killed. You are suffering with pain and missing part of your toenail.

Begin by connecting with the cells of your injured toenail in the physical world. Apologize for the pain and the hurt that you have caused. You could say, "I am sorry that you were damaged and I would like you to heal completely in the physical realm." Get the physical cells' permission to go back to perfect form and function.

Then you would access the divine template of the perfectly functioning toenail by stating these words. "I access my perfectly divine template of the toenail in Spirit. I ask the beautiful toenail cells in the divine template that are perfectly whole; to send their encodements to the injured physical part of my toe right now, including the damaged root cells."

Send the perfect encodements of the missing toenail from your divine blueprint in Spirit into the physical body. Command the cells of the toenail from Spirit to activate and implant themselves into the damaged toe, in divine order. Request that the divine template of the toenail transmit its perfect form and function into the physical toenail. Ask your damaged toenail to connect to the divine template and receive instructions to heal. Ask for the physical cells to become stronger, healthier and more loving than before. Let the physical toenail cells to come alive and return to perfect physical health. Give your body permission to heal.

You create a new template or program, from your divine blueprint to come alive in the physical dimension. The physical cells will react positively to the divine instructions. They just need to be told what to do and then they will lovingly do it. You must believe that this can take place. If the belief is not solid, there will be no paradigm for the healing to occur. You can do this with any cell in any part of your body. This is how you can turn physical dysfunction into function.

Chapter 29
VENUS

Lucifer is associated with the Morning Star, which is Venus, a planet long associated with earthmen and known for her beauty and higher resonance in the solar system. Venus is a warm planet, not rocky or terrestrial. It is considered too hot to sustain life. But life does exist there in the higher realms of consciousness.

Venus herself, broke off from the sun. When the sun was being formed in your solar system, the Mother's son gave birth to the infant Venus. This is analogous to the Creator giving birth to Lucifer. In your physical universe this relationship is represented by the sun and Venus.

The sun's rays are reflected in the warmth of Venus. The sun shines upon this most beautiful planet, and it is the brightest object in your evening sky. The beauty of Venus is truly unparalleled in your solar system. Souls go there to experience higher visions or revelations and to get closer to the sun.

In your mythology Venus is considered feminine, the sun is considered masculine. The polarities are reversed in the higher creations where the Mother Goddess is the Creator, and her firstborn is a son, a masculine being.

Many of those who have graduated from Earth School go to Venus. It is an intermediary place, a place where souls can advance. They can learn much about the laws governing the universe and how to create in the physical universe. They can learn about the science behind beauty, for example, about the golden ratio, golden rectangle and Fibonacci sequence.

Many great artists and architects from the past tapped into the Venusian energy in order to bring a divine stamp to their creations. They tapped into the noble truths of beauty. This was consistently done in the Greco-Roman world and by the great painters of the Renaissance.

Venus is instrumental in bringing creative ideas of thought into physical form. The Venusian energy transfers thought into form. It has highly benefited humankind because it has brought divine inspiration and ideas to Earth and grounded them here.

The builders and artists of the past who worked with this energy had Venusian energies, often times, in their astrological charts. They were able to be channels for this great energy of beauty and reform. It is the Venusian energy that rears up, that comes to the fore when Earth is to undergo great cultural changes in a positive direction.

This occurred in ancient times and during the European Renaissance. At that time the Venusian energy was squashed by dark forces, including the institutionalized Catholic Church. However, in the New Age, the Venusian energy will not be squashed. It will be allowed to expand and re-expand indefinitely. I will be instrumental in communicating and bringing the Venusian energy to the Earth, which will be fueled by the sun. If this sounds esoteric, it is just another way of expressing how energy is transferred in your physical universe.

There is a lightness and a playfulness to the Venusian energy. It is the only planet that can be seen from the earth, both in the morning and in the evening. Venus exalts the Earth and brings it to higher levels of understanding. I am guardian and custodian of this energy, as this was a post I held in the beginning, and it is a post I will resume in the Golden Age, so that Earth can more fully bask in the rays of the sun, bringing much radiance.

Chapter 30
HEAVEN

Heaven was my first home and I remember it fondly. There was much light and beauty in Heaven. And it became the first ground for creation. Many forms of life, many animals, elements, theologies, philosophies and the first ideas, were created in Heaven.

The remembrance of Heaven is contained within the human heart, and there is a direct link from the sacred heart of Jesus to the heavenly worlds. There is a passageway through the heart that will take you directly to Heaven, if you know the way.

Is Heaven a physical place? In some respects, it is because it is a place where angels dwell in incredible beauty and light. They play their instruments which were developed and designed in Heaven. They sing with their beautiful voices to God.

The frequency is complete peace and bliss. There is no yesterday, there is no tomorrow, there is only the beauty of the present moment. Your eyes and ears are enraptured in this vibrational bliss. You are bathed in that light, where one and all sing the praises of God.

There is no strife, war or bickering, as all are attuned to the heavenly frequency. That frequency does not allow for separation. When you look into the eyes of another, you do see yourself. You do not feel separated from that being. You are all as One.

There are many beautiful seascapes and earthscapes that can be seen in Heaven. The colors are much more vibrant and abundant. There are hundreds of shades of lilac, not just a few, and a hundred fragrances of lilac, each with their own particular variation.

The variety of Heaven is ongoing. As soon as you bring in one idea, thought or example into your mind, like a lilac flower, you can magnify the flower to see the circulation of the water running through its veins. Or, look at the flower from afar in a field and watch the communication between the heavenly bees and the fragrant flowers.

As soon as you look or study something, you become enraptured and go from point A to B to C. There is no boredom in Heaven. There is only learning and beauty, and the freedom to explore.

In the heavenly realms angels play. They gather to share joy and the laughter in their hearts, playing games and chattering without any ill intent. The communication is through the heart. Beings can read each other's hearts, as that is where the main point of existence lies. The minds are not predominant and one only has to gaze at another's eyes, to see the beauty that lies within.

There, many beings hold council. They discuss the evolution of various worlds. They can look at things visually, happening on the other side of the universe. They can bring their full attention to it, if they so desire.

There is no judgment in Heaven. Each being is allowed to pursue what interests them. The councils that govern worlds meet in special sections, so as not to disturb the abundant flow of love and joy.

Issues are discussed, problems are relayed and the heavenly beings make decisions to participate or not. Many heavenly beings, the angels and the saints, have come to Earth, directly from the heavenly realms to assist in the development of man and womankind, and to stave off evil. They do this out of love and devotion. It is a sacrifice for any heavenly being to come to the lower realms energetically, but this is what they do to bring about peace and reconciliation.

Heaven feels eternal and everlasting. When heavenly ambassadors travel to the worlds of light beings in the lower dimensions, it is always a special occasion and celebrated. When heavenly beings go to other stars and planets, they bring blessings, a manna, a darshan of heavenly love, so that other beings can experience and feel it – so that they can be uplifted.

Heavenly angels have the ability to descend into the lower dimensions and exist in different places, several places all at one time. Heavenly beings can replicate themselves, and be in many places at one time, in one moment. That is why people can call on the angels, and they can be right there, even though a thousand people may call on the same angel at any one moment.

LUCIFER RETURNS TO HEAVEN - A MESSAGE OF REDEMPTION

In Heaven, beings fly to get from one destination to another. Angels have beautiful wings that they use for transport. As they fall in vibration their wings disintegrate and fall off. It is a shutdown of the heavenly body. Of course, there is no sickness, pain or disease in Heaven. Everything can be created at a moment's notice. There is no dying, old or feeble age.

The offices of the personages in Heaven are highly respected. Angels love to serve and they feel intimately bound and loved by their Creator and brethren. It brings them happiness. When I was in Heaven, I was happy. I felt expansive, respected and loved.

I helped many and listened to all. I was a sounding board for many. I brought information and tuning to any being who requested it. I miss those days and the times that I helped the angels find greater peace, solace and wisdom. It was my job to help them expand in their essence, creativity and knowledge. I did this with zest and joy.

It is not to say that angels never rest in Heaven or enjoy solitude, because they do. I spent many a day resting near a rock on a lake, in a heavenly meadow, thinking about the best way to solve a situation, or misunderstanding among the angels. I still enjoy solitude to this day.

My job and goal is to bring Heaven to Earth, and uplift all sentient life upon the planet – life that has been demonically controlled for so long. Heaven will meet Earth. The hellish realms in the astral plane will transform into Light. I have seen that it is possible with good intention and a strong will. I will bring Heaven to Earth. Earth will be born into her heavenly and pristine self. The time has come for this.

Chapter 31
EPILOGUE - THE SUN

Your sun has a heart. As the sun beats its heart, the energies emit from the core and are transformed on the surface into hydrogen. Then they are released in a 360-degree movement into your solar system. Your sun is a star, one of trillions in your universe. A sun is an entity that collects beings around it, known as planets, who are there to find nourishment in the rays of the sun. The sun is a spiritual elder for these planets and its warmth and nurturance keep these planets evolving. The sun's energy makes it possible for the planets to evolve in their consciousness, and for the life forms upon these planets, to evolve. The sun is a giver of life and a giver of evolution.

There was a time in your reality when your sun did not shine. It was coalescing itself, bringing itself together, to form the light that it has now. It was amassing stellar matter to create a star, or sun. When enough matter amassed, the heart of the sun was born and the sun's energy got turned on by a higher force of consciousness. It got turned on by another sun and then the newly born sun, began to shine. This was a moment of promise and a moment of great celebration in your reality.

Your sun is connected to a tribe of other like beings, or suns, that carry the same or a similar frequency. They are connected by thought and luminosity. When one star in the network is fading, it is fed by the other suns. When a new star is to be born, the existing suns gather their energy and thought impulses, and send light and birth messages to the new sun. When a sun has finished its life, it will send out a distress signal, or an acknowledgment that it is going to pass form the physical realm of matter. It will send out a message that it is to die.

Then the sun takes off from the energy in its heart, and pushes it out and fully exerts it, until there is nothing left. This is called a supernova. And the supernova engulfs those planets that surround it and feed off of its energy. Those planets die as well because the sun and the surrounding planets are in a contract of life and evolution.

Many stars have been born and many stars have died. It is a long-life cycle, but a changeable life cycle. All great beings on your planet came to your planet via the sun. Their consciousness comes through your sun before they incarnate upon your planet, known as Earth. Before they come to Earth, they spend time communing with your sun, learning the ins and outs of evolution in your particular solar system and planet. The sun disperses knowledge, information and energy. It is a great resource for those celestial ones who sojourn to your planet.

The ancients knew of the power of your sun, partially. Therefore, they gave it great respect, as a giver of life. The ancients, the Hopi, and others, knew that they could gather information and remembrance, remembrance of who they truly were, by basking in the rays of the sun. The rays of the sun interact with physical matter in the human being, and if the individual is ready, codes of information will be turned on, that bring spiritual awakening and remembrance to the individual. This process has been carried out since time immemorial upon your planet.

I, in my higher form of consciousness, communicate with Earthlings using the power of the sun. In other realities I utilize other solar bodies. It is how I bring my consciousness to material form from spiritual form. The sun is a great transducer of energy. It is the go-between or the bridge between the spiritual and material realms. My spiritual body holds many suns and they all burn brightly within me. They charge me. They illuminate me. They bring me warmth and joy. My energy is cerebral, very mental, direct and powerful.

The sun holds many secrets of computation and energetics. It is beyond human comprehension at this time. As humans evolve, they will be able to digest and ingest more solar energy. This energy will be a teaching to them, expanding their mental bodies and their capacity to hold knowledge and understand information. The codes of life are held within the solar body. These codes make is possible for various life forms to exist upon your planet and others. These codes help to keep life in balance. Life is precarious and fragile. It is kept in balance by computations within the sun, that emit life-giving frequencies to various lifeforms upon Earth.

LUCIFER RETURNS TO HEAVEN - A MESSAGE OF REDEMPTION

The sun can and does emit different frequencies, depending on the lifeforms existing upon the planet. The rays and the energy it emitted during the time of the dinosaurs is different than the rays and energies that it emits now. In the future, it will also be different, as a new human race is born, with a higher capacity to live and learn. The sun will instruct those lifeforms. It will tell them how to live and how to be within their own physical organism.

Humans could not live without the warmth of the sun, but they could also not live without the codes of knowledge that the sun emits. When life was seeded upon your planet, it was seeded through your sun. And it will also die with your sun. So, veneration of this indispensable body is not archaic in the least. The ancients valued well that which gave them life.

Thank you for reading *Lucifer Returns to Heaven, a Message of Redemption*. I hope that you enjoyed it. I would greatly appreciate your review on the platform where you purchased this book. Reviews help to sell books. I would love more people to be exposed to the positive message in this channeled work.

To get on my email list, go to my website, lemuriandonnacarol.com. Scroll down to the bottom of the home page where you will see, "Join Lemurian Donna Carol's Email list!" You can sign up there. Thank you for your support.

Endnotes

1. There is only one spiritual truth for this reality at this point in time. This is not relative but absolute.

2. Prime Creator is a female who gave birth to Creation. She is Lucifer's mother.

3. God has no mind. God is energy that is channeled through the heart of a lifeform.

4. The Mother Goddess was the first entity that manifested out of the God energy, which was mindless. Lucifer was the second entity born from the womb of the Mother Goddess.

5. A dimension of Earth descended into a hellish realm after Lucifer and his angels fell. This was due to the separation from the God energy.

6. The Book of Life records all actions and thoughts in the multiverse. It is also known as the Akashic Records.

7. The reality of Earth is a hologram. People create in their mind and then manifest that reality in the outer world. However, the collective agrees to Earthly laws before incarnating here. This prevents chaos and provides order in this reality. Also, past-life karma and pre-ordained soul agreements or contracts are binding, until they are transmuted.

8. Akhenaten's soul mission was to create the Christ Consciousness grid upon the planet, originating from the Great Pyramid. This grid has been activated in current times and is necessary for the ascension of Earth and its inhabitants. Each lifetime of the Mother Goddess, starting from ancient Lemuria, had a specific soul mission that became a stepping stone for global Ascension, the great Shift of the Ages, that is occurring now.

9. Alcyone is the central sun in the Pleiades. Our sun revolves around Alcyone and receives transmissions from this central star. In this universe, the Mother Goddess and archangels live here.

10. Through the crucifixion, Jesus created a way for Satan to return to the highest light. This portal also opened to the fallen angels and fallen humans. Everybody has a way back home.

11. Judas Iscariot was complicit with Mary Magdalene's betrayal of Jesus Christ. He was a demon from Hell that had a cathartic conversion after Christ's crucifixion.

12. After Jesus Christ ascended, he returned to Earth. He started his life over again and wound up in Kashmir, India, where he passed.

13. The Arcturians are highly advanced humanoid star beings, from the Arcturus star system, in the Bootes constellation. Some are incarnated as humans upon Earth currently. As Earthlings, they tend to work in the healing arts and medical fields.

14. The Mother Goddess created the civilization of ancient Lemuria. She incarnated in Lemuria and brought many light beings with her. This was the original Garden of Eden.

15. While it is true that a human being is a fragment of God, a co-creator of their reality, we are not Prime Creator. We are limited by Universal Law in what we can create. It is a Luciferian doctrine that you are as God and can create like Prime Creator.

www.ingramcontent.com/pod-product-compliance
Lightning Source LLC
Chambersburg PA
CBHW072134160426
43197CB00012B/2098